Discerning Life Transitions

A SPIRITUAL DIRECTORS INTERNATIONAL BOOK

Discerning
Life
Transitions

Listening
Together
in Spiritual
Direction

DWIGHT H. JUDY

 Morehouse Publishing
NEW YORK · HARRISBURG · DENVER

Morehouse Publishing, 4775 Linglestown Road, Harrisburg, PA 17112
Morehouse Publishing, 445 Fifth Avenue, New York, NY 10016
Morehouse Publishing is an imprint of Church Publishing Incorporated.
www.churchpublishing.org

Cover design by Laurie Klein Westhafer

Library of Congress Cataloging-in-Publication Data

Judy, Dwight H.
    Discerning life transitions : listening together in spiritual direction /
    Dwight H. Judy.
        p.   cm.
    Includes bibliographical references (p.   ).
    ISBN 978-0-8192-2407-1 (pbk.)
    1. Discernment (Christian theology) 2. Spirituality. 3. Faith development.
4. Life cycle, Human—Religious aspects—Christianity. 5. Change (Psychology)—
Religious aspects—Christianity. I. Title.
BV4509.5.J83   2010
248—dc22

                                                                    2010021080

Printed in the United States of America

10 11 12 13 14 15   10 9 8 7 6 5 4 3 2 1

For the women and men
presently discerning ministries of spiritual direction
and for those who are seeking
the United Methodist Certification in Spiritual Formation

Contents

Preface

My life story has involved major shifts every ten to fifteen years within my career. These have usually been accompanied by changes in location as well. My wife, Ruth, has been a discernment partner for each of these changes. We've been surprised by some of our decisions. They have taken us to places we would never have imagined and to work that could not have been anticipated in our early twenties. Life has become a mystery journey for us. Since the mid-1980s, I have also worked with many creative people in midlife, seeking to discern new life directions. Perhaps the greatest surprise, as well as the greatest satisfaction in my career, was helping to create the nationally recognized United Methodist Certification in Spiritual Formation in 2000. As this book goes to press, I'm amazed at the many people with whom I've worked over the past decade who are now seeking this specialized form of ministry. I am constantly inspired by the wisdom of these women and men, as they articulate their unique ministries of spiritual guidance. This book would not have been possible without the courage, prayer, and dedication of the many individuals whom I have been able to accompany in vocational discernment. This book has been inspired by observation of God's dynamic work in their lives. In working with midlife adults in spiritual direction and spiritual formation studies, I have come to believe that all creative people will experience times of major transition in their life's calling, vocational direction, and family commitments throughout their adult years. We will seek to understand these changes together.

This book is for persons in discernment and for spiritual directors who accompany them. For me, the sense of life vocation or life calling is the broad theme that shapes our listening together in spiritual direction. I use the term vocation to mean our core sense of life purpose, which may reveal itself in multiple areas of our lives—through our commitments to family, friends, and community, as well as the more focused use of the term to describe our work life. I am always listening in a spiritual direction session for the underlying shifts in such core purpose. Our spiritual disciplines enable us to listen for such shifts within ourselves and one another. I have developed and used the reflective exercises of this book during my years of teaching and retreat leadership. These resources are offered to my colleagues in spiritual direction ministries for use in retreats, workshops, and individual encounters, with my permission. Scripture references frequently have brackets. These are either for gender inclusive concerns or to denote a more common usage than the translation used.

I wish to express my appreciation to the administration and faculty of Garrett-Evangelical Theological Seminary for a sabbatical semester, fall 2005, which created the spaciousness of time and easing of commitments, to begin this writing process. I am grateful to Nancy Fitzgerald, former editor at Morehouse, for her editorial suggestions; to Spiritual Directors International for their vision in creating this imprint; to Frank Tedeschi, senior editor at Morehouse; and to Joan Castagnone for the final editing of this book.

May these reflections prove beneficial to many in the quest for meaningful work and service, as well as in the quest for balance of family, personal, and vocational choices.

Dwight Judy
Garrett-Evangelical Theological Seminary
Evanston, Illinois
February 2010

Foreword

A Kaleidoscopic View of Discernment

Discerning Life Transitions is a resource for people in discernment of a major life decision and those who assist them. This is a book about personal vocation, the sense of *vocatio*, the inner voice. Vocation describes the core purpose of our life at a given time. Sometimes our personal sense of vocation finds wonderful congruence with the more common use of vocation to describe our work or career. Frequently, work does not complete us so fully. We may need to express our primary sense of personal calling instead through volunteer activities and community service, through caring for children, grandchildren, or aging parents. Perhaps we express our primary sense of life purpose through our charitable giving, gardening, or artistic endeavors. We may be entering a time of retreat, when our primary focus is our spiritual life, even while we continue to be engaged in work and family commitments. This core sense of personal calling will be balanced throughout our reflections with the other primary dimensions of our lives. Each of the chapters of this book focuses a different view on the discernment process. I like to think of these different viewpoints as comparable to turning a kaleidoscope. Remember your childhood joy in viewing the colored glass pieces through the turns of the kaleidoscope? Each turn showed a different pattern. As we work through the themes of the book, there will be a different glimpse on discernment questions like a turn of the kaleidoscope.

I hope the shifting patterns will also bring joy and surprise like that childhood toy. We could imagine the various dimensions that we will explore as dynamic, each interacting with one another as we turn the kaleidoscope and examine both our primary life calling and our many other ways of engaging life at this time of transition.

The following diagram illustrates the aspects of this kaleidoscopic dynamism. When one aspect of life is examined, others are affected. Each person enters the process of discernment from one or more of these areas. The discerner may be primarily concerned with questions of physical location—Where am I being called to live? Or with considerations for family members—How can I be more available for needs of parents, children, or grandchildren? Considerations may spring most directly from questions of career—Is my present job adequate for the person I am becoming or is it

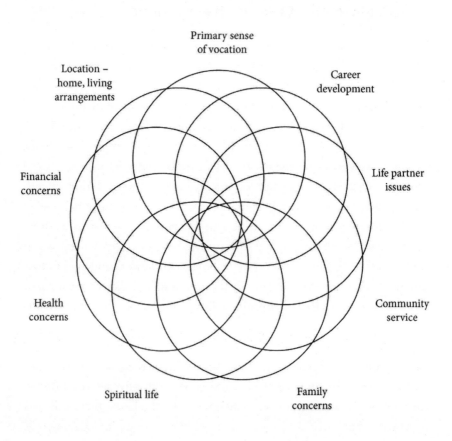

important to think of making a shift; and if it is, how will I accomplish this change? Or perhaps this is a time for examining my primary relationship or renegotiating my life partnership. Maybe health or financial concerns have interrupted my life, and I'm beginning to examine my priorities. We'll be assuming that in whatever way each of us enters the discernment process, all of these aspects will be shifting and changing through this time of life transition.

Perhaps your core theme is not shown on this chart. If so, adapt it, noticing how change in any one aspect of these areas will have an effect on the others. This time of life transition likely brings several of these arenas into focus. As we turn these various themes on our kaleidoscope, we look for new patterns of life to emerge that will be satisfying for this present time of life.

This book can be used by oneself, with one's spiritual director, or as a small group resource. The first part of each chapter provides discussion on particular themes relevant to discernment. These themes will be helpful to the discerner, to spiritual directors, and to small group leaders. The section of exercises at the conclusion of each chapter will focus directly on the discerner. Spiritual directors and small group leaders may want to suggest particular exercises for discerners. Here are some thoughts for each of these uses, beginning with the discerner.

For the Discerner—Attending to Our Day and Night Dreams

Each chapter concludes with themes for reflection and journal exercises. You may want to utilize all of the exercises for each theme or you may find only one or two of them to be significant for you. If you are working with a small group with these themes, you will want to be clear in your own mind which parts of your personal reflections are appropriate for sharing within the group and which are for you alone. You may be working through these themes with a spiritual director or other soul companion. Even in that relationship, some of your reflections need time to evolve and may benefit from sharing after some time of reflection for yourself. We have a wonderful gift in Christian tradition of the image of Mary pondering these things in her heart.[1] Sometimes issues are illumined by sharing with others, sometimes they are best kept within our own hearts for a while. I encourage you to trust which issues are best left within your own heart for a time and which are ready to be shared and discussed for further illumination.

If you have discovered this resource and are reading it by yourself, I encourage you to share some of your thoughts and reflections with a soul friend from time to time. The very act of putting our thoughts into words is often clarifying. We benefit greatly from communication with trusted companions while pondering such significant transitions in our lives.

As your thoughts begin to clarify, you'll note the very important principle of sharing your thoughts, your hopes, and your doubts with the people who would be directly affected in a life-changing decision. When you share these discoveries with people closest to you, what may at first seem an impediment can become the very gift of clarification that is most needed.

As you begin to look for your new vision for the future, your new hopes and dreams, do not be surprised if you also receive some significant night dreams as well. As you surround your discernment process with a sense of prayer and expectation, it would not be surprising if your night dreams become more active, dreams that may speak clearly to your discernment questions. Remember how often God speaks a message in the Bible through dreams. Joseph takes Mary as his wife because he is instructed to do so in a dream. He is instructed to flee to Egypt and to return to Nazareth in dreams. The other Joseph, found in the book of Genesis, is a great interpreter of Pharaoh's dreams, helping steer Egypt through a time of famine.

If you receive night dreams during this time of discernment that seem important to you, write them down with your other journal reflections. Listen for themes that speak from the dreams. A secret to receiving dreams is simply to place your journal by the bedside or to lie in bed for a few minutes after waking, inquiring about your dreams. The dream world is often eager to reveal itself to us. Sometimes dreams are very clear and obvious, others speak to us through images and metaphors. Another listening ear can be helpful in interpreting the guidance of our dreams. It will be particularly useful to take them for conversation with your spiritual director or another trusted companion.[2]

For the Spiritual Director or Small Group Leader

As spiritual director or small group leader, you will want to read this book in its entirety and think about the particular needs of your directees or small group participants. Critical questions are: How long can the discerners take for their discernment process? Does this work need to be confined to a few months like a season of the year? In this case, the book could be worked on intensely as one chapter per week.

If there is a major crisis at work for the discerner, spiritual direction sessions might be scheduled more frequently than the usual period of one month between sessions. There are ample exercises on each theme. Together as spiritual director and directee, you might determine which exercises for the period ahead might be most beneficial. Perhaps if you are working with a small group, the group would meet weekly. For the small group, attention to the assignments for the week or weeks ahead would be essential. It's also possible to use the resource more gradually. Perhaps this is a process that can be undertaken at a more leisurely pace. In that case discerners might work with the material at the pace of one chapter every two weeks or every month, so that *Discerning Life Transitions* becomes a companion resource for six to twelve months. Most major life transitions are at work within us for at least that long, so this may be a very effective tool for conversation, in addition to other themes that regularly come into spiritual direction.

As a spiritual director or retreat leader, you will find many specific themes and resources that you might offer on an individual basis to persons in spiritual direction or that you might want to adapt for retreat use. Most of these exercises have been utilized in small group or retreat settings effectively.

Working with a Small Group

Another way to use this resource is for a small-group study process. There are eleven chapters, each with multiple exercises. The first decision to make is how frequently to meet. While the material could be utilized as a resource for a group passing leadership from one to another, the material may be more easily handled if a designated leader assumes responsibility for the whole series.

For a small-group process, probably meeting every other week is the most desirable way to work with this book, although you could also choose to meet weekly or even monthly. You may want to utilize all of the exercises for each chapter or you may find only one or two of them to be significant for the group experience. In order for a small-group process to work well, there are a few basic principles that are important. Take a session to set your schedule and ground rules. This book has been field-tested with such a small group working weekly together. It was a very satisfying experience for participants. Many people found that the guided group discussion was extremely helpful, enabling them to share important themes within a confidential community. They related how uncommon it was to have a safe place to explore deep themes, such as contemplating a career change. They greatly appreciated the support of the small group to think through such important life transitions.

In working with a small group, you will want to establish a framework for sharing material that has arisen through the exercises of the chapter. Even if you have a convener, you may wish to rotate primary leadership each week. Such leaders need to be clearly designated. The leader could begin by reading the Scripture at the beginning of each chapter. After a brief period of silence, she or he could offer prayer. Each person might offer some reflection from the week that has been personally most significant. The challenge will be to determine the size of your group and whether or not all the participants can have adequate time each week to present the issues that have been at work within their own discernment. You will need to be very clear within your group how such time considerations will be handled. You may find that if your group is larger than six to eight people you should subdivide into small groups of about six each. That way, each person should be able to receive ten to fifteen minutes of group time each session.

Depending upon your group size and your group aims, you could keep such sub-groups throughout, or you may want to rotate as different small-group configurations each week. It's surprising how well a larger group can have a full conversation by doing this kind of rotation. Or you may wish to keep a large group of about a dozen or so people together, with the clear expectation that each time you meet a few of you will have more small-group time, rotating this carefully, so that over two or three sessions, everyone has his or her share of group time. A timekeeper is critical. Don't be shy about setting up a way of keeping time so that everyone has a turn. This can be as simple as setting a kitchen timer, leaving an extra two or three minutes for wrap-up, before moving on to the next person. Or you can rotate the timekeeping function, so that it doesn't become a burden on any one person. It actually fosters a climate of mutual care if the person who is speaking doesn't have to be simultaneously keeping too close a watch on the time.

When people share, they can speak what is on their hearts from the study material. They can relate experiences from the journal exercises or they may have an issue from the reading that they would like to bring to the group. In this case, they might wish to pose a question or to ask the group their interpretation of something in the reading section of the week. After their particular sharing, each person should also ask for feedback. What in particular would they like from the small group? It may be nothing. It may be a period of silence. It may be to ask for prayer or for a prayer from the group for the next week. There may be an issue that an individual would like to raise for group discussion. There might be one member of the small group whom the person sharing would like to ask for an opinion. In a group such as this, we are setting a prayerful climate of mutual care. It is important to let each group member set the tone for the kind of feedback she or he would like to receive. Sometimes what we need is only to share. Sometimes we gain insight just by speaking our thoughts. Or we might like to hear some others comment on whether they have had similar concerns with the content of the reading during another time in their lives. When a person's time is up, moving on is simple if the person who has just shared invites another person to do so.

At the end of the group session, leave a few minutes for summary. The leader can ask for general comments from the group, such as: What one thing stood out for you today? Again everyone may briefly comment. Or sometimes if your time gets very limited, you can ask all the participants to speak just one word about their experience from the time together. Make any arrangements regarding your next meeting, such as designating leader or primary people to share if you are a large group or how you will shuffle your small groups if you use that process. Close with prayer.

It is very important that your group establish mutual understanding about confidentiality from the beginning. I think the simplest form of confidentiality is to commit to not sharing any information with anyone who is not in the group. Individuals are working on very significant life issues through this discernment process. In order for the group to be utilized as a sounding board, it's critically important to have a climate of mutual trust. Over the course of these weeks, each individual may need to discuss their personal insights with people who are significant to them. In fact, that discussion of one's own emerging decisions is encouraged. However, they should not reveal the experiences of others in the group.

Some groups may wish to designate prayer partners for the duration of the discernment. Others may wish to have individual partners for sharing between sessions. Setting these basics can sometimes be difficult as people have differing amounts of time to devote to this process. However you set up your group, spend some time after about four sessions discussing these issues again to renew a clear sense of expectations together.

Near the end of your discernment, you're invited to make a plan and consult with any people affected by your decisions. Our discernment can never be complete without conversations with the people most affected. Your decision will necessarily affect family members and maybe a number of other people, who need to be brought into the decision process. As you move along through these exercises, if you begin to get a sense of major change that would affect significant people in your life, please start that conversation early and have it frequently along the way.

So, let's begin.

Notes

1. Luke 2:19.

2. Cf. particularly the works of Jeremy Taylor, such as *Where People Fly and Water Runs Uphill: Using Dreams to Tap the Wisdom of the Unconscious* (New York: Warner Books, 1992) and other titles. Also, for use of creative expression with dreams, see Jill Mellick, *The Art of Dreaming: Tools for Creative Dream Work* (Berkeley: Conari, 1996).

1

Introduction: Laying the Foundations for Discernment

We know that all things work together for good for those who love God, who are called according to [God's] purpose.

—ROM 8:28

Listening Together

Spiritual direction sessions take on many different patterns. Over time, an individual usually settles into a particular rhythm. Often in my experience as spiritual director, directees present an overview of life issues that have occurred since the previous meeting. In one spiritual direction session Todd[1] begins with this kind of overview of his life concerns. Todd is married, in his mid forties. He has worked as a consultant for ten years. In the spiritual direction session, he discusses different aspects of his work, prayer life, and relationships. With modest probing, he begins to relate options for a turn in his career. Suddenly, the energy of the conversation shifts dramatically. The air is almost electric or is it the presence of the Holy Spirit? Together the two of us sitting in holy conferencing realize that change is imminent. There will be a major turn in Todd's career. Many options open to him as possible ways to live into a calling that is more fully attuned with his current life vision. We have encountered what Meister Eckhart described as a "quick emanation" of the Holy Spirit.[2] It is a thrilling moment. We recognize God at work in our midst.

Much remains unknown. Many options are yet to be explored. Many consultations are yet to occur with his family and supervisors. Yet, we peer into the certainty of new life dawning. This moment comes after almost a decade of a life well lived, with clarity of call in his present career. This moment comes after seasons of conversation exploring dreams and hopes and creative impulses. It does not stand alone, but on the foundation of several years of searching for true calling, listening for divine inspiration, prayer, and conversation with significant people. The "quick emanation" rests on what Pierre Teilhard de Chardin called trusting in the "*slow* work of God."[3]

For Charlene, her discernment issues are quite different from Todd's. She keeps probing more deeply into her sense of life calling. Charlene has been divorced for five years and has two grown children. As she approaches the age of fifty, she's ready for more stability or a major change in her work as a health education consultant. She has often undertaken new jobs with great difficulty. She seems almost destined to move into demanding situations, requiring major personal sacrifices. Even when work flourishes, her supervisors do not seem to see a way for her to advance in her career. Over years of these difficulties she continues to pray and listen and discern. Her lack of external vocational clarity seems to make sense only as a path for deeper discernment of God's presence in each day. The "slow work of God" provides a continuing discovery for new opportunities. Our discernment task may be like Charlene's, finding new adventures in daily life in the midst of uncertainties.

This book is a resource for us to listen together for the "slow work of God," listening for that "new spirit gradually forming within us,"[4] and to help us recognize when the time is ripe for transition, when a "quick emanation" of the Holy Spirit is upon us. Images from nature can be used to describe this waiting and this time of change. "Throughout nature, growth involves periodic accelerations and transformations: Things go slowly for a time and nothing seems to happen—until suddenly the eggshell cracks, the branch blossoms, the tadpole's tail shrinks away, the leaf falls, the bird molts, the hibernation begins. With us it is the same."[5] As a resource for people in the midst of a major life transition, this book explores themes and offers exercises to explore more fully the decision process. As a resource for spiritual directors and for those in spiritual direction, this book offers a way to help us listen together for the movement of the divine creative impulse coursing through our life story.

In his book, *Transitions*, William Bridges differentiates "change" from "transition" and points to the common interchange of the two terms in ways that are not helpful. We can make changes in our life without making a true transition. Change for Bridges is about the externals of life, it is "situational." In his view, transition is about internal understandings, it is "psychological." Transition is "the inner reorientation and self-redefinition that you have to go through in order to incorporate any of those changes into your life."[6] We will utilize the term, life transition, in a similar way. We are seeking to understand external changes in our lives, but we are also seeking an understanding of inner transformations. We will point to the inward spiritual dimensions of the transition process as well as to practical realities involved in a major life transition. The very term discernment implies a stance that is multifaceted. We will work with biblical images of persons heeding a mysterious call to make changes in external circumstances of work, family, or location. While attending to this call, biblical characters often found that both their self-understanding and their understanding of God were also deeply impacted. In short, there is little sense of "change" apart from "transition" in the biblical stories. If we seek to follow God, we will be transformed in our very sense of self, in our relationships with others, and in our understanding of God. This task seems to be Charlene's present spiritual path. In spite of complexities in her career, she has clearly embraced the way of transformation through this time in her life. As Todd lives into the external changes he has begun, no doubt his inner resources will also be called forth.

As we look for the present focus of our life transition, Joseph Campbell's model of the hero/heroine's journey will be a key element in helping us understand the seasons or cycles of our life journey.[7] Based on Campbell's model, we will give prominence to seeking a primary life calling that is broad enough to encompass many different aspects of life. His model shows us that we tend to live with a primary sense of focus or life vocation for a period of time, often for several years. After this call's fruition, there may well come a time of boredom and restlessness, from which can arise a new sense of life direction.

Let us turn to Jeff's story to illustrate what Campbell described as finding a new "call to adventure." In midlife, struggling with his career as a parish pastor, Jeff decided it was time to reclaim a central part of his vocation as an artist. He discovered a position a thousand miles away, which would allow him to incorporate both his present career path, as well as his life as an artist. In spite of many obstacles, he sought out this job. Although he did not get it, making the decision to explore this possibility brought him great freedom. Jeff was able to reclaim his ministry from a different perspective and also find ways to renew his life as an artist.

Often, our discernment brings about similar surprises. Jeff's process of listening deeply within himself for clarity would well illustrate the path of inner life transition. Entering seriously into discernment will frequently bring a fresh perspective to our sense of inner calling. Vocation will be understood in our work in discernment in its broadest sense—from the Latin word, *vocatio*, a sense of "voice," of listening to the inner voice or inner calling and finding our own voice of expression and meaningful service for our present time of life.

As we look both to external changes and inner transformations, we will also seek to illumine multiple aspects of our relationship with God. Are the current structures of our faith adequate for the new sense of life calling before us? Does this new season of life purpose also require new perspectives on our spiritual life? A change in our faith or prayer life may itself become the catalyst for changes in other aspects of our lives.

The call to Abraham[8] and Sarah helps us to recognize times when we vaguely know a period of life has ended, yet the pathway to a new beginning is not yet clear. How do we discover the new sense of life calling or the new "call to adventure"? There is a magic moment in the movie *Indiana Jones and the Last Crusade*. As Indiana Jones nears the grail cave, he finds himself standing on a ledge, thousands of feet high, with nothing below. He recalls an image from his father's diary, and summons the courage to step off into nothingness. But he lands on a bridge, enabling him to walk across the chasm. There are times when we too must step out before the path appears. This issue of trust is well described in the message God gives to Abraham, "Leave." There is no clarity of destination when the time for leaving is first revealed.

I first experienced such risky leave-taking in my mid-thirties. I had enjoyed parish ministry for almost a decade when suddenly tasks that had been meaningful became empty. My inspiration had departed. I described this time saying, "My soul has left and I need to find it." I had to step into the unknown. I did not do it very gracefully at that time. But, I did step forth and found a new life. And I prayed that I'd be able to observe times of such completion and the need for new life direction more clearly in the future. As we work with people in spiritual direction, we often need to assist them to leap with care into unknown circumstances. As discerners of our life process, if that call to change is summoning us, it is an important time to reach out for companionship in spiritual direction or to journey together in a covenanted group into the unknown.

This book is designed to help us search well and fruitfully for that next step of life, work, relationship, or place, when the previous era is ending and the way forward is unknown. Usually, there is not a ready source of external support for thinking through such issues. Our Western culture is so externally focused that it is very difficult to find conversation partners when we are wrestling with major changes. It is even more difficult to find places of support and safety to discuss those inward transformations that may be pushing through to our awareness. It is a rare joy, then, to be able to companion one another through the spiritual direction relationship during such times of inward and outward reorientation.

Attending to our Commitments, Limitations, and Hopes

We each live in a vast web of relationships and commitments. These commitments are to be honored and further revealed in times of transition. I prefer to examine these relationships and commitments with the challenging term, "obedience," because it puts our commitments into very sharp focus. All of us have made both conscious and unconscious vows to certain individuals and to particular core values for our lives. We live in obedience to these significant vows. During those times of life when we explore major shifts in our life stories, these commitments often come into conflict with each other. In working through the themes of this book, we will seek to clarify our vows of obedience to spouse, if so partnered, to family members, to our own soul's callings, to society, to place, to friendships, and to God. When the stirring for new life begins, we will need to reexamine these ultimate commitments. How can they move us toward new life, even if we perceive some of them to be in deep conflict with one another? By taking these conflicts of commitment seriously, we are able to examine the tensions from which new life will emerge.

An assumption I bring to this work is that, as we honor all of our commitments, there will inevitably come moments of impasse when it does not seem possible that a way can open. I am equally committed, however, to the premise that by leaning into these deep challenges a creative way can open for us. This kind of impasse may well bring us to the humility of spirit in which God can most effectively offer us breakthrough possibilities.[9] Particularly in times of impasse, we may need to discover new ways of waiting for revelation. New resources of prayer and companionship may be required of us. Neither rush the decision process nor hold back when clarity emerges. Attending to all domains affecting our decision process is critical. Having the hope that clarity will emerge is essential. Having understanding companions with whom we can share these hopes, dreams, and difficulties is invaluable.

We will draw on Daniel Levinson's understanding of "life structure" to assist us. Most of us experience sustained periods in our lives when these multiple commitments work well together. Levinson describes these times of stability as "advancement within a stable life structure."[10] We can readily understand this concept when we think of the period of child rearing as a family. Hoping for stability during the time of our children's movement toward maturity, we minimize the number of major moves so ties with friends, community, schools, and family can be established. In such periods of stability, we also hope for sustained productivity within our careers. These are the times when our creative spirit is well used, when our careers and finances advance. Yet, we know that different life patterns and commitments will arise when children move onward with their own life journeys. Perhaps coincidentally with less attention needed on the home front, it is time to consider career shifts or changes of location as parents of grown children. In seeking to understand our current creative urges for new life, we have the benefit of much research on life transitions and adult life stages. It is often clarifying, when we are confused about our life purpose, to ask how many of our difficulties are ours alone and how many of these struggles are the result of a predictable pattern related to our current life stage. Life looks very different from the perspective of making the first important career choice of young adulthood than it does with a midlife career shift or the quest for life purpose after retirement. Each life stage brings its own challenges. We are beneficiaries of more than a half-century of reflection on life stages as well as their unique impact on women and on men. Our reflections will work with the unique life stage themes for young adults, midlife adults, and senior adults.[11]

We each also have limitations. For some people, there are limitations with conflicting commitments to self and to family. For others, there are severe limitations of financial resources. The global economic and environmental crises in recent years have thrust many people into a period of examination of vocation and living circumstances. These undesired predicaments may serve as catalysts for entering a period of discernment regarding life goals, vocation, and living arrangements. Sometimes such external crises can bring us face to face with hopes for our life purpose, which we have been neglecting.[12] Sometimes, there are limitations from deep struggles with self-confidence. A time of attention to issues of inner healing or forgiveness may be necessary before we are free to listen deeply for our life calling. For most of us, there will be times when external social or economic forces present major obstacles. We may believe that we are clear regarding next steps in our life, yet external reality intervenes. A promised package for retirement does not materialize; the family home does not sell; there is a disruption of health; death comes to a close family member. At such times, we must return to the foundation of our discernment process: What are we ultimately seeking? For the work of discernment, a particular Scripture has become bedrock for me. In the concluding section of the book of Philippians (4:4–7) St. Paul writes:

> Farewell; I wish you all joy in the Lord.
> I will say it again: all joy be yours.
>
> Let your [generosity] be [known] to [everyone].
>
> The Lord is near;
> have no anxiety,
> but in everything make your requests known to God
> in prayer and petition with thanksgiving.
>
> Then the peace of God,
> which is beyond our utmost understanding,
> will keep guard over your hearts and your thoughts,
> in Christ Jesus. (NEB)

Even after Paul postulates several conditions prior to offering our prayers and petitions to God, the answer to our prayer is not the immediate fulfillment of a specific request. Rather, the answer is a living relationship with the "peace of God." What we receive most of all in this amazing venture with God is a deepening clarity of relationship, as Paul describes it: "the peace of God . . . keep[ing] guard over [our] hearts and . . . thoughts in Christ Jesus." What we receive is *wisdom*. We receive hearts and minds molded and taught in the ways of life and love. What we ultimately receive is the assurance that God is with us, regardless of the way our life changes evolve. The stories of Charlene and Jeff, as they search for fulfillment in their careers, point clearly to this possibility.

For all persons then, regardless of outward circumstances, let us make the bold affirmation that there is hope. There can be a vision for life lived fully aligned with our own natural skills and character, while also serving the good of the world. We are made for meaningful service and deep relationships. Whether single or partnered we are made to create our homes, as the medieval marriage ceremony proclaims, to be a "haven of blessing and a place of peace." We are made for love and service. Toward what creative venture with God are we now being called?

Season for Discernment

Living through times of major life transition is hard. Discernment of major life decisions may take a year or two. Often, however, there is a precipitating event that causes us to seek completion on a decision process over a few months' time. Much of our work as spiritual directors is to listen faithfully with others for their nudges of creative movement into new life patterns. As spiritual directors, we do our work well only if we continuously attend to that same deep question: In what ways is the creative God leading me? All of us live through many stages and transitions over a lifetime. Yet, in all cases, a process like the seasons of the year is at work. There are beginnings. There are times of growth and development. There are times of completion and harvest. My experience in working with people over many years is that we are not so well prepared for the in-between times as for living within one of the seasons of growth or harvest.

One of the greatest difficulties in life discernment processes is learning to wait for God's timing or the aligning of the many forces and individuals at work in any life change. We may have one agenda for change. God and life circumstances may well have another. Because of my many twists and turns in such life decisions, I've come to appreciate the necessity of clarifying our vision for change and waiting until others discover a similar vision. After experiencing several of these in-between times, I have come to affirm this essential period of waiting as a time to allow the Holy Spirit the opportunity to act on our behalf. We live in a vast web of interactions with many individuals, as well as with God. We do not always experience a timely alignment of these many forces and people to bring about the desired outcome. In the work of discernment we look to one another to maintain hopeful spirits, while we await clarity for our decisions.

I have had the privilege of working with midlife women and men for thirty years in a variety of settings. Many were seeking a shift of vocational focus. Many were engaged in graduate school studies. Others attended retreats or were seeking a new passion for service through spiritual direction. My own life journey has taken many turns. I now look back on these life decisions as marking significantly different eras. My career is a testimony to God's creative spirit. In no way could I have predicted the major turns of my path. At each point, I have been invited into a dramatically different opportunity, which I could not have anticipated in my young adulthood. I began my career thinking I would move into seminary teaching early on. Instead, I was engaged in parish ministry for almost a decade, then directed an off-campus graduate studies program, and later became a retreat center director. Ironically, I will end my formal career as a full-time faculty member in a seminary, teaching spiritual formation, a field which was not articulated for Protestant seminaries when I began my ministry in the late 1960s. Each major change has been marked by much effort on my part as I tried to attend to the deep disquiet in my spirit when a career task seemed to be complete. In those times, I sought out information for new directions and entertained options carefully. Many of these options did not come to fruition, yet they were very important to explore. Finally, often from a completely unexpected source, the new direction came. I've now grown accustomed to such times of deep vocational discernment as being marked by grace. But, even after going through such major shifts at least four times in my career, I approach the "next" with a sense of mystery, as well as anxiety. Once again, I am engaged in this process, now nearing formal retirement. In our discernment process, let us look together for the "slow work of God" gradually forming within us, as well as those moments of clarity, the moments of a "quick emanation of the Holy Spirit."

As we approach our inner longings, we will benefit from exploring several key themes:

- Discerning personal calling
- Seeking images from Christian tradition and Scripture that help us in discernment
- Sorting out commitments to spouse, to family, to self, to the greater good of the world, and to God
- Managing financial obligations in light of pending change
- Completing tasks of our previous era of life with grace
- Finding the grace and energy to leave parts of our old life structure
- Making the time for honorable endings
- Celebrating a time of jubilee or sabbatical space in between major changes

Preparing the Way for Listening

We know that all things work together for good for those who love God,
who are called according to [God's] purpose.
—ROM 8:28

This book is designed to help individuals reflect on and pray over one or more major life decisions. We will do so in the context of affirming that "all things work together for good for those who love God, who are called according to [God's] purpose." In Philippians, Paul speaks of prayer being answered with the "peace of God." How do we wait until this peace appears in our hearts with regard to this decision? If all things do "work together for good," how do we cooperate with this divine process? Each time we enter into discernment regarding major life decisions, we may find ourselves questioning the adequacy of our faith and seeking a new kind of relationship with God.

Much thought is usually required to make the radical affirmation with Paul that "all things work together for good." This statement applies to those who love God and who seek to live according to God's purpose. The invitation from these texts is that along life's way we will be given wisdom to see how God seeks to bring about good in all things. These great statements do not suggest that everything in life is good or easy or comfortable. Instead, they suggest that, as we continue to love God, as we continue to have our dreams and hopes shaped by God, we can come to see life through God's hope for goodness for the world. Our perceptions of who God is and what is good for us and all persons concerned in our decisions must be malleable. We must enter into a posture of willingness to be led. Is it possible, indeed, for all things to work together for good for all the billions of people on the earth? For all created beings? What is the role of one individual in such a grand scheme? How important is my intentionality toward cooperation with the whole of existence? In a meditation on the decisions of Ruth in the Hebrew Bible, Carolyn Stahl Bohler suggests that it is possible that all people can make "right" choices along their own unique life paths. "Imagine all people making right choices" is a phrase within a longer guided meditation, entitled "Along Life's Path."[13] Bohler invites us to entertain the grand notion that all people could simultaneously make "right" choices for themselves and also be in concert with others in their choices.

Is it possible that all things can work together for good in our lives if we love God and live according to God's purpose for us? How might our life decisions be impacted by such an affirmation? I ask you to hold a stance for this present work in discernment that affirms both your own intentionality and effort and yet is open to the unfolding of grace in surprising ways. Sometimes it is the spiritual director who holds this hope for others when it seems all but impossible for all things to work together for good.

The first part of our discernment may simply be no. The first clear message that a new sense of life purpose is coming may arise from a sense of the negative. The only thing that may be clear is that we can no longer continue in our present situations. Perhaps we've entered a period in which we keep hearing ourselves say, "I can't do this anymore." The no to a current pattern of living is emerging. As spiritual directors, our role is often to hold faith for our directees, to hold the belief that change will come and will be for the good. Jeanne Achterberg writes powerfully of the time after she is diagnosed with cancer on the eye and before healing treatment is possible. She writes of the importance of engaging others to hold trust for her, because there will inevitably be times when she cannot keep trust herself that healing will come.[14] Our role as spiritual directors is to hold that trust for people when they are entering the unknown of discernment. Frequently we must face the struggle of ending a phase of life before the new pathway is clear. As persons in discernment, it is most helpful to seek a small circle of people in addition to our spiritual director to hold that sense of trust for us.

The yes of our discernment often takes some time to emerge. While waiting for clarity, we may discover that it is very important to pay attention in new ways to small joys and simple ways of exercising our creative spirit as we begin to build the foundation of new life. It may also be very important to discuss this sense of changing life focus with our supervisors at work and with our loved ones at home. Surprising turns of events can occur when we become clear that a certain way of living or working must come to an end. My most significant lesson in this area came during the previously mentioned time of confusion in my mid-thirties when I was struggling with the sense that I was being called away from parish ministry.

I had gone from Texas to a training experience in California. During the training, I discovered a graduate program that began to speak most directly to me. As I talked with my wife, Ruth, on the phone, I said, "I think I've found it, but we have to move." Ruth replied, "Didn't you realize I've been ready to leave for two years?" Well, no, truthfully, I'd been so caught up in my own struggles for vocational clarification that I had not been listening well to Ruth's equally difficult discernment process. Her reply set in motion our plan to make the move, which we accomplished within a year. Close friends and family members can frequently see directions for us more clearly than we can for ourselves.

Listening with Prayerfulness

Over the many life transitions I've experienced, as well as in the process of listening to many people in life transitions, it has been very helpful to look at the balance between "effort" and "surrender."[15] We must lay our own groundwork for the transition. We must explore options, sometimes sow many seeds, examine our financial and educational capacities and our relational commitments. Yet, we will discover that a posture of openness of spirit is also required. That openness will allow us to receive possibilities that we could not imagine on our own. We can think of this polarity of effort and surrender as the attempt to live the principle of "Thy will be done," not passively but with fierce intentionality coupled with flexibility. We could also call this posture in listening for human longings in such times of major life transition by the term, "prayerfulness."[16] In his writings on prayer Larry Dossey uses the term prayerfulness when confronting health issues. For Dossey, prayerfulness blends human effort and surrender. In the midst of severe illness, our challenge is to pray for a positive outcome, yet also to seek the highest good for all concerned. Prayerfulness enables us to live into the surrender of "Thy will be done," while continuing to offer our hopes for the person in crisis. I invite us into an attitude of prayerfulness for our discernment, offering our best hopes for positive outcomes for ourselves, yet also yielding into the greatest good for all concerned. Openness to surprising new pathways we could not envision for ourselves is essential.

For the Discerner

In the following brief exercises, we will form the foundation to which you can return as you work through the discernment themes of this book. Perhaps you'll want a new journal just for this purpose.[17] Or you may work on your computer making notes. Perhaps you have a trusted journal process and will continue with that.

As we lay structures of prayer and reflection around the discernment work, we will often be surprised at the readiness of our inner world to reveal itself to us.

Let us begin with that great affirmation of faith:

We know that all things work together for good for those who love God, who are called according to [God's] purpose.

I. Discernment Themes

The following questions may help you to begin your discernment process:
- What theme or themes do you bring to this process of discernment?
- What details are necessary to know in order to discern the outcome?
- What are financial implications?
- What are implications for family members and friends?
- What kinds of decisions would you need from your employer in order to approach these issues clearly?
- What image or images would describe your present emotional and spiritual relationship to this discernment issue? Can you draw it or find a picture to illustrate this image?

2. Spiritual Disciplines for Discernment

What spiritual and physical disciplines would be useful for you to observe during this time of major life decision? Please note that the suggestion of "daily" can primarily be an intention. We seem to get very good results if we interpret "daily" as four to five times per week. Even so at this time of significant personal reflection, the intention of "daily" can be very comforting. Please check those that are most appealing to you. Watch out for your guilt trips, thinking you must do all of these! Be playful. Select those which you think will nourish you well. Revisit this list a week after you've done it and make appropriate adjustments.

___ Daily prayer time	___ Weekly prayer time
___ Daily journal time	___ Weekly journal time
___ Daily Bible reflection	___ Weekly Bible reflection
___ Daily physical exercise	___Weekly physical exercise
___ Daily creative expression	___ Weekly creative expression

___ Regular conversation with spiritual director or trusted friend

___ Regular conversation with small group of people in similar discernment mode

___ Reclaiming one "lost" talent from a previous era. Name this activity, designate how you will reclaim it and how often.

___ Visits to geographic areas of interest. Are there areas you want to explore as potential places to live in this transition or in the future? Are there places you've wanted to visit for inspiration? Name those and make a calendar of possible times.

___ Regular contact with nature

___ Regular worship

___ Retreat for one or two days at regular intervals. Specify how often and where.

___ Visit to art museums, attending musical events, fairs, festivals—specify how often and where.

___ Visits with significant people in your life from past and present. Name individuals you would like to visit, themes of conversation. Designate when you'll be able to accomplish this.

3. Just for Fun

What is one thing you will do each week just for fun? This can be very simple, such as going to lunch with a friend, taking a walk, going to a movie.

Name it _____   Schedule it _____

4. Practicalities

What information gathering, budget planning, conferring with others, etc., will you do in the next few weeks with reference to your discernment?

Make a list. Start an information file.

Notes

1. All stories are based on encounters with individuals or composites of several persons, but for the sake of anonymity, names and circumstances have been altered.

2. Matthew Fox, *Breakthrough: Meister Eckhart's Creation Spirituality in New Translation* (Garden City, NY: Doubleday, Image Books), 363.

3. From a letter to his cousin Marguerite Teilhard, July 4, 1915, in Pierre Teilhard de Chardin, *The Making of a Mind: Letters from a Soldier-Priest, 1914–1919*, trans. R. Hague (London: Collins, 1965), 57.

4. Ibid.

5. William Bridges, *Transitions: Making Sense of Life's Changes*, 2nd ed. (Cambridge, MA: DaCapo Press, Perseus Books, 2004), 4–5.

6. Ibid., xii.

7. Joseph Campbell, *The Hero with a Thousand Faces* (Princeton, NJ: Princeton University Press, Bollingen Foundation, Inc., 1949; second edition 1968).

8. Gen 12:1. "Leave your own country, your kinsmen, and your father's house, and go to a country that I will show you" (NEB).

9. Note the first of the Beatitudes: "Blessed are the poor in spirit, for theirs is the kingdom of God." Matt 5:3 (RSV).

10. Daniel J. Levinson and others, *The Seasons of a Man's Life* (New York: Ballantine, 1978), 150.

11. Erik H. Erikson, *Identity and the Life Cycle* (New York: Norton, 1980); see also Erik H. Erikson, *Life Cycle Completed, Extended Version with New Chapters on the Ninth Stage of Development by Joan M. Erikson* (New York: Norton, 1997) and Carol Gilligan, *In a Different Voice: Psychological Theory and Women's Development* (Cambridge, MA: Harvard University Press, 1982, 1993).

12. The popular press is beginning to report people making major career changes in the midst of the economic turndown of 2008–9. For example, see Chase Snyder, "Changing Direction: Mike Miller, 30, is one of many in this area who is using the economic downturn as an opportunity to better themselves," Working Together section, *Goshen (IN) News*, February 17, 2009, 15–17.

13. Carolyn Stahl Bohler, *Opening to God: Guided Imagery Meditation on Scripture* (Nashville: Upper Room Books, 1996), 62.

14. Jeanne Achterberg, *Lightning at the Gate: A Visionary Journey of Healing* (Boston: Shambhala, 2002).

15. I am indebted to one of my important teachers, Frances Vaughan, for this theme. In a class in 1980 in which I participated in my doctoral studies, she asked us to ponder the question, "Did you primarily get to where you now are through effort or through surrender?"

16. Larry Dossey, *Healing Words: The Power of Prayer and the Practice of Medicine* (San Francisco: HarperSanFrancisco, 1993).

17. Some discerners may wish to explore journals using visual or kinesthetic practices. There are a wealth of such resources now available. Keywords for such book searches are "art journal" or "art journaling." Also, see Betsey Beckman and Christine Valter Painters, *Awakening the Creative Spirit: Bringing the Arts to Spiritual Direction* (New York: Church Publishing, Morehouse, 2010).

2

Destiny and Calling

The Lord said to Abram, "Leave your own country, your kinsmen, and
your father's house, and go to a country that I will show you."
—GEN 12:1 (NEB)

One day Carol's husband said to her: "You're not the same person you used to be." In her mid fifties, Carol had been in her executive leadership position in a corporate setting for five years when she had this conversation. She had begun this position with great enthusiasm and vision. She was surprised with her husband's comment, but she also understood the truth of his observation. She received his comment as a summons to review whether or not her current employment was still compatible with her life calling. After a period of reflection, Carol decided to leave her position and seek another.

In her early sixties, Nancy's bishop asked her to stay one more year as a supervising pastor, instead of retiring as she had been planning. After a health crisis, she decided to stick to her original plan to retire and focus her energies on "listening to the songbirds, watching the seasons change, and dwelling with the Holy One."

For a number of years, Jim held a contract position with a major university. But, beginning in his late fifties, it was unclear how long his position would continue. His next step would be retirement from full-time employment. With a formal retirement date uncertain, he and his wife began to make a set of serious alternative plans, if he was asked to leave his work before he was personally ready to do so. After the crisis passed in his early sixties, Jim found himself struggling for clarity about when he would want to set the retirement date. Even so, he appreciated his new sense of freedom, wondering at the potential of living more freely day by day as a time of preparation for a now elusive retirement date.

Fran's career path began surprisingly early. She had a math elective that she needed to take for high school graduation. Without much forethought she took an accounting course and discovered that she really enjoyed the mental stimulation of accounting. Several years later, as a CPA, she took a position in a major accounting firm. There she met the man who would become her husband. Fran and her husband have continued their work as accountants through their forties.

We encounter each of these people at profound turning points in their life stories. In addition to career choices or shifts in our inner lives, family circumstances often bring about times of profound change. Each life stage can change our sense of self and life calling. Whether we have children early or later in our adulthood makes a great difference in how we look at our lives. When our parents may need our assistance in elder years, and how much they may need us, will affect our choices. Frequently when one or both of the partners in a marriage make a major career shift, there is a need for a profound renegotiation of the relationship. The central task may become working out new understandings of their relationship through counseling. Sometimes we are compelled to make a decision that puts us in direct conflict with one or more people who are very important to us.[1] Sometimes we can make such major turns in our life story and be blessed upon our way by those in our immediate circle of relationships.

Our present life stories are often as intriguing as stories from mythology or Scripture. The Book of Ruth tells of a time of famine when the widows, Ruth, Naomi, and Orpah, must decide where to go and live for the rest of their lives. They must choose a new sustaining community. As a mature man of power and wealth, a gnawing sense of incompleteness in relationship to his wronged brother forced Jacob to return home and make amends (Gen 32). In the Holy Grail stories we encounter Perceval, who as a sixteen-year-old boy, witnessed five knights passing through his village, left his mother, and became a wandering knight himself.

Whether we draw on personal experience or from biblical and mythical stories, one of the most important aspects of human existence is that from time to time a new era of life emerges. This shift can be prompted by inner longings, such as the desire to live more fully in a sense of "dwelling with the Holy One," or by discovering unexpected skills. A new era can announce itself through an outward circumstance, such as bereavement, a serious health crisis, the pending empty nest, or a company downsizing or an unwanted early retirement. The calling can come when someone else identifies a sense of purpose for us, which we had not known how to name ourselves. The summons to change may come from deep within, as a new sense of personal self-understanding emerges. For some people, a new way of relating to God can bring about radical questions regarding vocational or relationship choices. Our life calling in such times may be to devote our primary energy to our inner life through prayer, retreats, counseling, or spiritual direction. Sometimes outward circumstances of work and family can be maintained during such times of inward calling. For some, a sabbatical may need to be negotiated in order to devote oneself deeply to the inner call.

Destiny?

> For it was you who formed my inward parts;
> you knit me together in my mother's womb.
> I praise you, for I am fearfully and wonderfully made.
> —Ps 139:13–14

As we listen to our present discernment questions, we usually find ourselves face-to-face with the question of destiny. To what degree am I completely self-creating? To what degree is my life path deeply embedded within the structures of my family, social, and cultural circumstances? There seems to be an abiding mystery at work within us. How does one human being develop a unique personality, with a particular set of talents, interests, genetics, and family circumstances? Is there a particular destiny for each of us? Have we, indeed, been known by God in the womb,[2] before any other circumstances intervened? Some believe so. James Hillman seeks to describe the unique destiny of each human being as the "acorn theory." He speaks of this inner consistency within our life journey as our relationship with the inner *daimon*, our core life force as described in Greek mythology, or our guardian angel. Just as an oak tree is embedded in the acorn, so our life destiny is ours from the beginning of life.[3]

While we may or may not make such a strong affirmation of this principle, most of us can see patterns of consistency to our life decisions in retrospect. From time to time we must wrestle again with this inner *daimon*, or guardian angel, to continue living creatively. To what degree is a sense of destiny for particular life work and relationship patterns given to each of us? To what degree do we create our own callings or destinies? While we each have unique gifts, talents, and inner callings, we also seek out education and mentoring in order to be equipped to answer that call of inner destiny. As we find ourselves living into different phases of life, how is it that our fundamental sense of calling also shifts? How is this sense of particular calling and destiny also at work beyond our conscious choices and seemingly guiding us in different directions from time to time? Do we live as if "that which we are seeking is also seeking us?"[4] Whether young adults making their first career and life partner choices or midlife adults reevaluating those first choices or elder adults shifting their focus for life energies yet again, it is profoundly important to look for that inner thread of fundamental character and calling within ourselves.[5]

As young adults make their first and very important steps toward vocational calling, it can be very helpful to hear from elders who have had a variety of different jobs over the span of their careers. For some, those jobs seem quite disconnected from one another. For others, there is a very strong common thread throughout the career path. When I reflect on my own vocational journey, I see great continuity. From the standpoint of an objective observer, it probably seems as if I've had five or more different careers: parish pastor, therapist, retreat leader, academic administrator, program director of a major retreat center, seminary faculty member, and spiritual director. From my perspective, there has been more commonality than difference in the variety of ways of expressing my creative ministry. Each vocational task has equipped me more fully for my present work in the field of spiritual formation, which I would not have known how to name or claim when I was making my first stab at career calling. Hillman would say I have been in communication with my inner *daimon*, that mysterious element of soul which cannot be easily described. Often I have not known how to name a certain sense of dis-ease that has descended upon me when my outward life no longer aligned with my inner sense of soul. I have usually been like Carol, the corporate executive, with whom we began this chapter. I, too, have needed help from others to begin to name a shift in my priorities. My wife and others close to me have noticed when I have lost some of my humor or have become too obsessed with work issues. By pointing out that something was not right, these individuals helped me to begin listening more carefully for a sense of shift in my life direction.

One of the gifts of thinking of external life as being in communication with a more mysterious sense of depth is that it puts our times of discomfort into perspective. If indeed there is a *daimon* seeking to live creatively from our deep soul, it only makes sense that from time to time we will be out of synch with this deep essence. It may be time to listen to our discomforts, our passions, and our frustrations and inquire if these messages from the depth of our soul are seeking to communicate with us. Sometimes we can easily answer a call for a new direction. At other times there are very demanding financial and family commitments to which we must give first allegiance, and we must find a way to stay in place in our career, even while we listen inwardly for a new direction.

The great danger, however, is that we ignore these signs and begin to do damage to our health or to the quality of our relationships. Jeff, the pastor introduced in the first chapter, was inspired to look for a position in which his sense of self as an artist could be expressed. His example illustrates one of the most important aspects of discernment within a time of life transition. It is very important to follow leads that speak to neglected aspects of our life, such as Jeff's expression in art. Although a change of job did not take place, Jeff had a radical change of perspective and found a way to honor his much-neglected life as an artist. During this time of discernment it's very important to pay attention to our places of dis-ease. Spiritual directors are especially adept at noting areas of dis-ease in our words and asking the probing questions that help point us toward what our deep soul essence is seeking to express to us. Together, let us enter into conversation with the eternal element within ourselves and the struggles to express true calling within our particular potentials and limitations. We can pose this task another way: Can we let our "life speak," as Parker Palmer has so eloquently suggested?[6]

Shaping Destiny with Reality

In the mid-1980s Beverly Potter wrote an intriguing book on career development. Now in its third edition, *The Way of the Ronin* postulates a very interesting thesis.Using the image of the Japanese medieval ronin she describes a career path that has virtually become normative for us. A ronin was a samurai warrior who was cut loose from his obligation to a feudal lord. When, for whatever reason, he was no longer able to give allegiance or receive support from a lord, he had to find various causes with which to align himself. The ronin was a warrior on his own. Potter made the very astute observation that in our times, we cannot usually count on the kind of lifelong security from major corporations that was the hallmark of American life in the mid-part of the twentieth century. Our corporations no longer resemble feudal lords, guaranteeing us lifelong jobs and retirement security in exchange for company loyalty. This change of culture cuts across economic and social boundaries. Our culture increasingly has adopted the way of the "ronin" as a preferred way to employ individuals. Outsourcing is but the latest of such trends.

Many of our churches are struggling to operate from the old paradigm of lifelong commitment to denominational structures, while seeking to deal with issues of clergy competence and family needs. The global financial crises of the first decade of the twenty-first century have led to enormous difficulties for countless people, forcing them to face the tasks of renaming and reclaiming essential life purpose. We have virtually all become "ronins," and have sometimes been ill-equipped to face the entrepreneurial demands that life has placed before us.

In such a time of job insecurity, Potter proposes that the most "secure" job path is that of embracing the way of the "ronin." On this path, we do not expect job security, but continuously prepare ourselves for an evolving career path by following our own deep interests and skills. Our skills change over time. We develop our interests and capacities in new ways. We are able to say yes to opportunities that stretch us. We basically accept the job insecurity of our times and allow that very insecurity to open us to new callings from within. The challenge with the "ronin" way is that it depends upon one's own initiative. It is an entrepreneurial path, a way in which we must continuously seek a new story in which to live and serve. It is a pathway that ultimately enables us to make creative new contributions to our world's needs.

Abraham and Sarah: Heeding the Call to Adventure

It is no accident that Abraham and Sarah are held out as the progenitors of faith for the Middle Eastern and Western worlds. This story, at the heart of Jewish, Islamic, and Christian Scriptures, offers us the archetypal way for listening to deep shifts and changes within our life stories. It has often intrigued me that so many people want assurance from God in a way that is far clearer than those assurances given to people in Scripture. We have *the* story to understand how God also speaks to us today in the story of Abraham and Sarah. Do we want to have God talk to us directly, as God talked to the people of the Bible? Then, we should start with Abraham and Sarah.[7]

What is it that Abram heard when he was seventy-five years old?[8] How did the message of God appear to him? With one simple directive, "Leave!"[9] Carol, the corporate executive mentioned at the beginning of this chapter, heard such a summons when her husband told her that she was no longer herself in her current position. We can imagine Abraham inquiring further. "Well, OK, if I am to leave this land in which I have lived my whole life, the land of my ancestors, where am I to go?" And God answers, "You will go to a land that I will show you." Hmm. This is not exactly a clear road map, is it? Perhaps much of the difficulty we have in hearing God is that we want too much. We want clarity that it is not in the nature of God to give. We want a map. We want a specified direction. We want security. And what God gives instead is an adventure in which we have the opportunity to know more fully who God is, what human life is, and who we ourselves are. We only get the assurance that God will be "along the pathway" with us when we undertake such an adventure. What we get is a relationship with God and self rather than a clear-cut answer. Even if it is filled with insecurity, isn't that answer of relationship with God ultimately much more fulfilling than a specific onetime answer would be?

As we consider our current discernment themes, I invite us to reflect on our life stories, perhaps remembering a time when the only thing we knew was that it was time to "leave." And didn't we resist at least for a time? Wasn't it just too uncomfortable to set out as Abraham did? Even if there was some strange promise like that given to Abraham's wife, Sarah, that she would bear a child in her old age. Even if there was some vague hope of creative renewal, such as that promise to Abraham that childless as he was now, his offspring would one day be as prodigious as the stars of the sky? The awareness that a time of life has ended, that a season is finished, is one of the most critical ways God speaks to us. We ignore that message of no to our present circumstances to our great peril.

I received that first no when a pathway to graduate studies did not open early, as I had assumed. Instead the pathway opened for almost a decade of parish ministry, while further graduate studies dimmed in my interest. A much more difficult no came near the end of my nine years of pastoral ministry. I had grown deeply committed to that vocation. I often spoke of the various tasks of parish ministry as being hand in glove with my own potential through which I continued to grow in creative ways. But, rather suddenly, I was in discomfort. Previously inspiring tasks had become repetitive. I noticed that I was frequently angry for no apparent reason. I was bored. I was receiving that call of God to leave. I had no idea such a deep calling was at work. I had not experienced such a divine no before. I did not know how to respond. Yet, when I did begin to respond to various creative nudges, a new way opened. A mystery journey began. Listening to this deep discontent led me and my wife into doctoral studies. At the time, for us, we surely felt as alien in our move from Texas to California as Abraham and Sarah did when they first set out in response to God's call. When we can finally get clear that we are hearing God's no to present life circumstances, we must face a life-altering decision. Will we be able to accommodate the no and still live creatively in place or must we embark on a major change? If we can do so consciously, in either case, we begin what Joseph Campbell describes as the "call to adventure" of the hero/heroine's journey. A new life unfolds. And the next time (and the next and the next) that such a season of change descends upon us, we are perhaps better equipped to listen for the changes and embrace them.

In the pattern of this hero/heroine's journey, illustrated below, we hear an interior call or a divine message, much like that of Abraham and Sarah, and set out to answer the call to adventure. Then we encounter unknown forces, often facing severe tests. But, there are also surprises of helpers along the way. We learn much in this new arena. Often, we are literally in a new place or a new job or a new family circumstance. We have much to learn in this new adventure, because we have not been in these circumstances before. Once the goal or prize has been attained, there is a return to the world to share the wisdom we have learned.[10]

Jacob's is one of the most complete stories of the hero/heroine's journey that we have in the Hebrew Bible (Gen 25–37). Jacob becomes the preeminent model for the individual before God. Jacob is ornery. He is motivated by greed. He is, in short, everyman and everywoman in the quest for success in the world. Nevertheless, he also is blessed by God with a sustaining vision for his wilderness journey. His call to adventure begins when he attains Esau's birthright by stealth. After he steals that birthright, he must flee into the wilderness. That is his threshold crossing. He has left his familiar world behind and must seek a new land. He is sustained in the wilderness by his vision.

After twenty-one years in the land of his uncle, he has attained the "prizes" to be gained there: his wives and children, his herds and wealth.

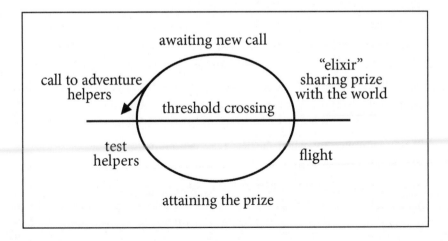

Finally, he completes the hero/heroine's journey by returning home to make peace with his brother Esau. Because of his tenacity on his solitary journey, he is given a new name, and made the model for all Hebrew history. His wrestling match with the angel is his threshold crossing of return. Jacob is so tenacious in demanding a blessing for his individual uniqueness that he is given the blessing in the form of a new name. His name is changed from Jacob, which means grabber, to Israel, because he "strove with God and [humans] and prevailed" (Gen 32:28, NEB). Jacob is the model of tenacious honoring of our individual callings before God. He is given the name of greatest honor within the history of the Hebrew people. Jacob's story becomes the clarion call for the Hebrew quest for personal freedom and responsibility before God.

This story is played out over and over again in Scripture. It is Abraham's call to the unknown. It is Sarah's call to motherhood. It is Ruth, Naomi, and Orpah's call to seek out new communities of support during their bereavement. It is Job's call to faithfulness in the face of devastating loss. It is the young Mary's call to motherhood. It is Jesus' call first to his teaching/healing ministry and then his call to the cross. The New Testament church is born of the call from bereavement at the crucifixion and the bewildering array of postdeath appearances of the risen one. The model of the hero/heroine's journey is a powerful lens through which to interpret biblical stories. Through this model we see the ultimate prize of human existence—the discovery of an evolving relationship with God that can endure our many changes of life circumstances.

Sometimes, the call comes as a surprise encounter that moves us into a new life venture. A new direction may suddenly appear to us. Such a call appeared for Daphne in her forties. Daphne had worked for years in a university. She did not have the sense that she was called away from this work, but instead would find a way to integrate her new calling in spiritual formation. She was in a spiritual formation program, following her impulse to develop her inner life, when she heard her denomination's order of deacons described for the first time. She had not known there was a way to integrate her present training and life path with her sense of how God was calling her in attending to her spiritual life. Her immediate response was, "Wow! I didn't know you could do that. This is just what I've been searching for." Now, several years later, she has completed the training necessary for ordination as a deacon all the while continuing in her full-time job. The so-called "secular" and "religious" domains are no longer separated in her life.

Let us be open to such surprises!

For the Discerner

As you begin to explore the new summons calling you into this season of discernment, let's turn to the cycle of the hero/heroine's journey. It can be very helpful to look at this cycle as unfolding in different ways for the different domains of our lives. Often, there is a particular cycle of the story playing itself out with our lives as parents, if we have children. Can you not remember the radical change in your life upon the arrival of children? There can be a different cycle playing itself out with regard to a particular job. Our marriage relationships can be on yet another cycle. Often the deeply challenging aspects of managing our time and commitments can be illumined by discovering whether or not there are conflicts within these different domains of our commitments. Because my wife and I had children in our early forties, in the midst of rebuilding our careers after the hiatus for doctoral studies, my mid forties were a very difficult time for me. The competing struggles of parenting infant children, while also focusing strongly on career proved very demanding. My wife's challenge was perhaps even greater, as she was also the primary family support for her mother, whose health was declining. All this, while my own work life required me to travel a great deal.

So, indeed, both Ruth and I can claim that name given to Jacob, that of "Israel." In that era, we both had to learn a lot about perseverance, striving with God and enduring. There are inevitably times when such deeply competing commitments emerge in our life stories. Let us call these competing commitments arenas of obedience. We have made ultimate commitments, for example to partner and to career or to family and ourselves. Sometimes these arenas of obedience put us into such deep conflict that it seems as if there is no way through. Naming these arenas of potential conflict can be very helpful. Trusting that God will provide a way through is essential. My personal testimony is that such breakthroughs do come. A way opens before we see it.

As you view your present life story through the cycle of the hero/heroine's journey, I invite you to begin by focusing on one area, the one that is most prominent for you now. Utilize the model of the hero/heroine's journey to help you name this particular life pattern. Take one hour at the beginning to think through the particular themes and make notes. Return to these issues over the next week or two. Later, you'll look at another area and examine possible areas of conflict between the two arenas of concern. Let's look again at the basic pattern.

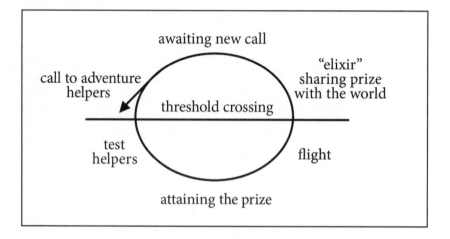

Arenas for Consideration

1. Work/Vocation

   Where are you in your cycle of satisfaction/achievement within your work? Has your work or economic stability become insecure as a result of the recent economic crisis? Do you need to consider a new call in your work? Use the model to explore "tests" but also to think creatively about "helpers" who might assist you now.

2. Immediate Family

   How are your children progressing? Where are you in your relationship to your spouse, to your family development? Are you in a new cycle with aging parents?

3. Personal Spiritual Life

What is your cycle of adventure with regard to personal issues of growth and development? Have you "plateaued?" Are you awaiting a new call to adventure?

4. Health Issues

Have you or family members had to deal with major illness? Where are you in that journey toward recovery?

Now, pick one of these four areas (or another of your choosing) and work through the following questions that arise from the hero/heroine's journey. Write your life story "as if" there is an inner destiny that you have been fulfilling. Can you name the character of what Hillman calls your inner *daimon* or trace your acorn development?

I. Your Life Adventure

- What is the present call to adventure in this arena? Sometimes this is easy to name, sometimes it is not. If you find yourself in that situation, go on to the other questions, and then come back to this after you've thought about these issues further.

- At the threshold of change, what are your blessings? What are the difficulties? Do you have a "vision" of where you're headed, even if the specifics are not clear?

- What or who pose current "tests" for your adventure? (The tests often appear as particular individuals with whom we're having difficulty. They may also be trying circumstances that we can't seem to solve.)

- Who or what are, or might become, "helpers" in the adventure? (One of the wonderful themes of Scripture and mythic stories is that in every new adventure, there are always new helpers. Helpers can be real people we learn to reach out to for support. Helpers can also be new ways of prayer or a new circle of support.)

- What is your image of the success of this adventure? Be as specific as you can about your "picture" of yourself in being fulfilled in this adventure.

- Are there challenges for the threshold of return? Often people who have made major interior changes or have set off on a new career path in midlife have difficulty in getting their new skills put into real world jobs. Or on the family front, perhaps you and your spouse are facing the "empty nest" and having difficulty returning to life as a couple. In mythic and Scripture stories, this challenge is frequently posed as "flight," a very demanding time to take what has been gained back into the world.

- How do you envision sharing what you've learned into the life of the world? That is called "elixir giving." It is our ability to share what we have discovered, to use our talents for the health of the greater community. We are not fully satisfied until we can do so. Are you encountering difficulties in doing this kind of elixir giving? What would it look like to be able to do so?

After you have made notes on each of these, perhaps a "title" to this adventure will emerge for you. Or you may revisit what you've written under the call to adventure and amplify what you've written there. Can you locate where you are dwelling in the story right now (call to adventure, threshold crossing, approaching the prize, claiming the prize, seeking the return, return threshold, elixir giving, awaiting new adventure)?

2. Write about Your Adventure

   Write a fairy tale or a story about your adventure. You can begin, "Once upon a time," if you like. You can utilize animals or magical creatures. Afterward make any notes about what else you discovered about this call to adventure.

3. Choose a New Adventure

   After a week or two, pick a different arena from those listed above or from your own life experience and repeat this process.

4. Consider Your Adventures

   Spend some time thinking about your two stories. Do conflicts arise for you by being concurrently involved in the different cycles of these two stories? What are areas of seeming impasse to competing arenas in which you have given a sense of ultimate obedience? How can this exercise help you better understand some of your current frustrations? Frame a prayer to help deal with the impasses you can name.

5. Write a Letter

Read Psalms 139:1–18. Write a letter to yourself from God before your birth, while you were forming in the womb. Describe the destiny that is given to you for your life work and relationships. Discover if there are tasks yet to come that God would like for you to complete before you die.

6. Just for Fun

What is one thing you will do in the next few weeks, just for fun? This can be very simple, such as going to lunch with a friend, taking a walk, going to a movie.

Name it _____ Schedule it _____

7. Practicalities

What information gathering, budget planning, conferring with others, etc., will you do this week or next with reference to your discernment?

Study your previous list of practicalities. What needs to be carried over? What do you want to add? What do you need to add to your information file?

Notes

1. Joan Andras, "A Phenomenological Investigation of the Decision-process of a Woman Trusting Herself in Making a Spiritual Commitment That is Contrary to the Wishes of a Significant Person or Persons" (PhD diss., Institute of Transpersonal Psychology, Palo Alto, CA, 1993).

2. "My frame was not hidden from you, when I was being made in secret, intricately woven in the depths of the earth" (Ps139:15).

3. James Hillman, *The Soul's Code: In Search of Character and Calling* (New York: Random House, 1996), 5-9.

4. Paraphrased from statement of unknown origin, "That which you are seeking is also seeking you."

5. Note the subtitle of Hillman's book, "*In Search of Character and Calling.*"

6. Parker J. Palmer, *Let Your Life Speak: Listening for the Voice of Vocation* (San Francisco: Jossey-Bass, 2000).

7. Gen 12–25.

8. Abraham, originally called Abram, is renamed Abraham ("father of generations") when the promise of a son is given. Sarah, whose original name is Sarai
(meaning "mockery"), is renamed Sarah ("princess") in this promise. See Gen 17.

9. Gen 12:1 (NEB).

10. Diagram adapted from Campbell, *Hero with a Thousand Faces*, 245.

3

Longings and Life Structure

We do not know how to pray as we ought, but that very Spirit intercedes with sighs too deep for words.
—ROM 8:26

Listening to Longings

You may recall Jim's dilemma concerning retirement plans introduced in the previous chapter. Let's begin our theme of "longings and life structure" by hearing more from him. For several years, Jim's primary daily discipline has been his morning walk, which has also become a time of prayer and reflection. A short daily walk for him is about two miles; if it is possible he prefers a three-mile walk of about forty-five minutes each day. On one such walk during vacation in the Colorado mountains, Jim acknowledges a deep longing beginning to arise. Now in his early sixties the longing has become a familiar sense of unease. He has learned to notice this sense of disquiet after several major shifts of location and vocation through his life. Change is beginning. This time he knows that he will retire from formal employment over the next few years. To mark this change externally means thinking about finances, living arrangements, and connections with friends and family. There are obvious reasons for his discomfort and longings, particularly as they are accompanied by anxieties regarding the financing of retirement. But, during his walk in the mountains, Jim wonders if there is a deeper level of concern arising in him. In Hillman's words, his *daimon* is trying to speak to him. He notices a lessened capacity for long hours of detailed work and tries to pay attention to his frustration when a day brings a nonstop barrage of e-mails to answer. He longs for space for his mind to wander into the terrain of new ideas. He wonders if there is a shift from "doing" to "being" happening from within. If he could find a way for a more spacious daily routine, would there be more joy and creativity in his life?

Early in Jim's life story, it would have been unthinkable to focus each day from a sense of "being" as opposed to "accomplishing." It is a radical and frightening thought to presume that his life might carry the same sense of worth and meaning if he could no longer count his accomplishments each week. Yet, he now knows it is very important to pay attention to this inner shift that seems to be occurring. Can he trust himself not to slip into the deadly sin of *acedia*, or sloth, ceasing to be truly engaged in the world? Perhaps, he thinks, this inner shift may be a new spiritual task, learning a different way to engage his sense of social responsibility and work life. Our popular society gives little help for these retirement considerations. The culture seems to say, "You've served your time, now it's time for you to play." Yet, those senior adults who are well adjusted in their retirement or in extended work into their late sixties, seventies, and eighties seem to have a different attitude—that of a conscious sense of meaningful service. Clearly, for Jim, as Hillman would affirm, it's very important to listen to the disquiet, even as he longs for more of the quiet sense of daily "being" for his life.

From the beginning of his career path, the opposite of this polarity of being and accomplishing has been Jim's experience. Always, he has approached his work with accomplishing—with doing. As a result, he has struggled throughout his working life to regain balance by taking time for recreation, rest, retreat, and vacation. And now, as he observes the surprises of wildflowers popping up where he did not expect them and finds simple pleasure in the stirring of a gentle breeze, he wonders if there is actually a calling coming forth to organize his life around aspects of being—prayer, appreciation, making time to dwell daily in a spirit of generosity—rather than living with a sense of urgent duty. He makes note of these surprising ideas, as they are clearly one way to describe the yawning chasm of change that looms before him.

On the other hand, Janet, a woman in her late forties, speaks of too many years of "being," too many seasons of frustrated efforts to find a vocational niche, of being forced into daily self-creation for a sense of accomplishment with no outward affirmation. Now she is ready for a season of "doing." She finds the answer to her longing through a new vocational call and an exceptionally demanding job in graduate teaching that requires her to focus her attention outside herself. She relishes the increased pace of life that these new tasks bring.

After years building a successful career, another midlife woman, Maggie, acknowledges a deep inner disquiet, a growing desire to shift into a new career. She does not anticipate a change of pace of life, but rather a shift of vocational focus. But, Maggie finds it very difficult to share this deep longing in her workplace, where she is seen as a success.

During times of discernment, it is very important to listen carefully to our discontent. A very helpful Scripture helps us to consider the power of our longings and discontents:

> I consider that the sufferings of this present time are not worth comparing with the glory about to be revealed to us. For the creation waits with eager longing for the revealing of the children of God. . . . We know that the whole creation has been groaning in labor pains until now; and not only the creation, but we ourselves, who have the first fruits of the Spirit, groan inwardly while we wait for adoption, the redemption of our bodies. For in hope we were saved. Now hope that is seen is not hope. For who hopes for what is seen? But if we hope for what we do not see, we wait for it with patience.
>
> Likewise the Spirit helps us in our weakness; for we do not know how to pray as we ought, but that very Spirit intercedes with sighs too deep for words. And God, who searches the heart, knows what is the mind of the Spirit, because the Spirit intercedes for the saints according to the will of God.
>
> We know that all things work together for good for those who love God, who are called according to [God's] purpose. . . .
>
> —ROM 8:18–28

This Scripture shows us many of the profound themes with which we wrestle in order to create a meaningful life. And I suggest these great themes rear up, particularly in times of life transition, to be dealt with afresh. The Scripture invites us to enter our time of life transition with these affirmations:

- It is possible to love God and determine God's purpose for our lives.
- Our own intentions can cooperate with God's work of continuing creative renewal of the world, human society, and creation.
- We can wait with patience for these revelations.
- The inarticulate groans or "sighs too deep for words" within us are messages from the Holy Spirit and can help us discover the purpose of God.

Young adults are very aware of these deep inner groans of the spirit. Their vocational and relationship choices are perhaps more difficult because of these uncertain times. Yet, we really lose nothing and perhaps gain everything if we trust that through listening well to the longings of our hearts, we may actually be listening for divine guidance. In times of great disequilibrium, the creative renewal of social and economic life may be even more possible than in times of relative stability. Suppose amid massive layoffs and economic uncertainty, people responded not simply by trying to find a job similar to the one they've lost, but by listening deeply for the creative inspiration within themselves as they renew their careers. As Psalm 84:6 affirms, then "the valley of Baca [tears]" might become a "place of springs." At such a time, we may be encouraged with Pierre Teilhard de Chardin's advice to his cousin in her time of discernment:

> Above all trust in the *slow* work of God. We are, quite naturally, impatient in everything to reach the end without delay. We should like to skip the intermediate stages. We are impatient of being *on the way* to something *unknown*, something *new*. And yet it is the law of all progress that it is made by passing through some stages of instability—and that it may take a very long time. . . . And so, I think it is with you. Your ideas mature gradually—let them grow, let them shape themselves, without undue haste. Don't try to "force" them on, as though you could be today what time (that is to say, grace and circumstances acting on your own good will) will make you tomorrow. Only God could say what this new spirit

gradually forming within you will be. Give Our Lord the benefit of believing that his hand is leading you surely through the obscurity and the "becoming", and accept, for the love of him, the anxiety of feeling yourself in suspense and incomplete.[1]

While it is extremely difficult to be in a position of "waiting," there is also opportunity for a deeper stirring of God's movement within. Let us all listen well to the heart's visionary longings for a world enhanced through our lives and work, while also being attentive to the very real concerns of making a living and caring for our families. How can this time of upheaval become an invitation to new ways of prayer and new understandings of the love of God? Above all, how do we allow ourselves to continue to be inspired with hope, regardless of changing life circumstances? Do we believe that we are called by God for meaningful service in each season of life and in all circumstances of our world?

Life Structure

A very helpful way to examine our longings, the inarticulate groans of our hearts, is to have a sense of "where we are." Daniel Levinson's notion of life structure helps us to do just that.

A number of years ago, in preparing to lead a men's retreat, I pulled a book from my bookshelf I had not read in several years, Levinson's book, *The Seasons of a Man's Life*.[2] I was amazed at the wisdom contained in the book. Levinson lifts up a concept that I have found very helpful. He describes what he calls "life structure." We all have a life structure at any given moment of our existence, one composed of our physical and social living arrangements. These include the nature of our homes or apartments, our neighborhoods, our shopping patterns, and people with whom we regularly interact. Life structure includes family arrangements. What is our marital status? Are children at home? Are parents or grandparents nearby? Have we reached an age in which parents are in need of much care? Are parents deceased? How do we interact with people in our neighborhood?

We expand our understanding of life structure in describing our work lives, exploring such themes as our job satisfaction and stability, our commutes, our sense of economic stability, our opportunities for advancement. Young adults reflecting on these questions can ask if they have the necessary information and resources to make their first major career choice.

Life structure also includes our sense of community, our connections with friends and family, and our connections with the places we live by participating in a church, service organizations, or volunteering. Are these connections adequate for us; do we have a good sense of social connections or are we in need of cultivating new connections and friendships?

An area not included by Levinson, which I would add is what I would call "faith structure." After we locate ourselves within a life structure, turn to the question of faith structure. As we face a time of discernment, we may well find that there is a dislocation in our sense of spiritual resources. We can inquire into the adequacy of our spiritual communities, our prayer practices, and our spiritual beliefs. We may discover that this is a time for exploring new understandings about God. Just as we are listening for longings for our life that might evoke external changes, so we can also listen for inner longings for a greater sense of divine presence and guidance.

This concept of life structure helps us describe the geographical setting in which we live. Our life structure means that we have a particular set of economic circumstances; our work life has a particular configuration; our family life takes on a unique character; our religious self-understanding and expression have unique forms; even our relationship with God may have a special character at a given time. Our longings and groanings of spirit can be illumined by our present life and faith structure.

Outcomes of Life Structure

Levinson utilizes the concept of life structure to illustrate the stability or instability of our lives at a given time. He writes of five possible outcomes for a particular life structure:

- Advancement within a stable life structure
- Advancement that itself produces a change in life structure
- Failure within the life structure
- Breaking out—seeking a new life structure
- Unstable life structure

Advancement within a Stable Life Structure

Hopefully, we have all experienced periods of relative stability. Our jobs are reasonably satisfactory, we have stable families and finances. In such circumstances, we are able to "advance" on professional and personal fronts. We have a satisfying season of growth. We are able to live into "hope for things not yet seen" and actually experience some of those hopes coming to fruition.[3]

Advancement That Itself Produces a Change in Life Structure

This pattern, I suspect, occurs less frequently now than in that era of job stability of earlier generations. It can, however, still come with an increase in work responsibilities. The classical version of this issue occurs when one is moved from frontline work to management. The individual may find the burdens of middle or upper management unsuited to her temperament. And although salary and prestige benefits may be substantial, the question of life calling may loom again.

The growth of children and aging of parents fits the pattern also of "advancement that itself produces a change of life structure." Once our children have progressed through the normal stages of development, the time comes when they are no longer so dependent upon us. Family life changes and we must adjust to these changes. We may need to care for aging parents. Or we may find ourselves in the privileged position of being able to provide stability for other family members experiencing difficult times. To provide a stable center for others will cause us to make necessary adjustments in our life structures.

Failure within the Life Structure

The natural calamities and economic failures at the beginning of the twenty-first century have disrupted life structures. For some, these disruptions have resulted in death, destruction, and a call for the creation of completely new life structures. For others suffering less obviously, there may have been disruptions to a sense of normal life for a period of time. Perhaps a severe health crisis has caused "failure within a stable life structure." Suddenly, with the onset of severe illness, a whole new life understanding demands an inevitable shift of priorities. Struggling with disease becomes the uppermost concern for the family. Economic difficulties may also ensue.

An unwanted "downsizing" also creates a major crisis. Even when we anticipate such realities, the termination can be overwhelming. Many people are reeling from the economic downturn that began in 2008 and have suffered major dislocations. A normal retirement can also be destabilizing.

Breaking Out—Seeking a New Life Structure

"Breaking out" can be very exciting. Those who retire successfully experience the exhilaration of breaking out. They have the financial resources and life skills to relocate or to carve out a new lifestyle. Frequently, people in midlife go back to school, training in a new vocation. The exhilaration of new learning and new colleagues creates a new sense of vocational calling. A major issue for those breaking out may be a financial one. Levinson reports that it may take as long as fifteen years to regain the financial level and recognition in a new profession. Nevertheless, those persons who break out are very much like those archetypal progenitors of faith, Abraham and Sarah.

Is there some inherent creative unrest for those whom God calls? Perhaps there is an ongoing call to new creation, which is irresistible for some. Economic concerns and the question of a place to call home become secondary to the need to respond to the inner calling for new creation. Extraordinary difficulties call forth our deeper dreams and hopes as we begin a new life, even if it is thrust upon us.

Unstable Life Structure

Individuals without a sense of stability experience major difficulties. A young adult may not expend the energy required for the creation of a career that could provide stability. Mental disorders are certainly destabilizing. Addictions may prohibit development of practical skills. In such circumstances, the basic need is to create a sense of stability, to build both a foundation of income and a sustainable living situation. If we are ourselves experiencing a time of great instability, we may need to take advantage of society's safety nets in order to take the time to find a renewed sense of stability. For years people have paid unemployment insurance through state taxes. It may be very important to collect from these funds while seeking employment or taking an opportunity for training to shift vocational direction.

Outcomes of Faith Structure

We can also apply Levinson's analysis to the issues of our faith. Do we have an adequate "faith structure"? Is it serving us in a satisfying way? Are we able to experience sustained growth within the practice of our faith? Are there serious discrepancies between the practice of faith in a religious setting and our soul's longings?

Perhaps our faith journey has reached a plateau. Do we nourish our soul with practices such as prayer and meditation? Have changes of worship style left us bereft of hallmarks with which to celebrate our faith? Do we have an adequate community of friends and fellow seekers for life understanding? Has our experience outstripped our understanding of God? Is it time for a reorientation of our concept of God? An intriguing way to demarcate the adequacy of our faith structure is to ask how long it has been since we deeply grappled with our basic theology. Usually, we will have periods of relative adequacy of our sense of personal theology in which we can "advance within a stable faith structure." Such a pattern may last for several years. Perhaps, instead of stability, this is a time to "break out," to become a searcher after a new understanding of God and of our faith practices.

No matter if the hurricanes of life have intervened, either literally or figuratively, a stable life structure may have been so disrupted by disaster, health, economic, or relationship concerns that we have been forced into a time of profound questioning of our faith. Who is God in the midst of this difficult time? Where is God? As the writings of the saints attest, there often comes a time when God seems absent after a period of sustained presence. What happens to our practices of faith as a result?

As we think on our faith structure, we will gain insight by differentiating our faith into five areas: (1) intellectual construct of God, (2) practices of faith, (3) relationship to faith community, (4) coherent sense of personal meaning, and (5) felt sense of God. Any of these five aspects of our faith may change. Change in one arena may bring about change in another area. For example, as we and as our faith community experience change, we may come to the point that there is no longer congruence between our heart's needs for spiritual nurture and the way that a particular community expresses its faith. Or we may have wonderfully sustaining relationships within such a community of faith that outweigh the shifts and changes within such a community over a number of years.

Advancement within a Stable Faith Structure

We can apply the same general categories to faith structure as Levinson applies to life structure. Perhaps we are experiencing "advancement within a stable faith structure." There is congruence between our practices of faith and our external life structure. We have adequate practices of faith and a community of faith to nurture our spiritual development within the demands of our life structure as shown in work and family relationships. There is relative stability for us and a sense that things are "working together for good," both in our inner life and in our outer life.

Serious Breakdown or Disruption of Our Faith Structure

Perhaps we've entered a time of profound disruption of our faith structure. Our cultural norms expect that in times of crisis our faith will provide a foundation for us. Our faith structure is supposed to contribute to our sense of stability when all else is faltering. But that is not always the case. For example, suppose our life structure has been stable enough that deep unresolved psychological scars have now come to the surface. Suppose the pain of this process shakes the foundation of our understanding of God and prayer becomes very barren for us. There is no stability in such a time of deep personal crisis. And we are ill served by people offering platitudes to sustain us. Instead, it may be more honest and helpful to acknowledge that there are times when there is a "serious breakdown or disruption of our faith structure." A time of deep searching may follow. People may need to leave their community of faith in order to look deeply into their own hearts. It may be an extremely lonely time. Perhaps there can be a new community of searchers with whom to share the struggles. Perhaps such a time will enable a person to reach out to find a spiritual director or pastoral counselor to help in articulating her or his faith understandings and practices in new ways. This profound sense of faith disruption may be very difficult to explain to family and friends—a reality that only deepens the sense of loneliness and abandonment.

Advancement That Produces a Change in Faith Structure

Perhaps we have experienced advancement within a faith structure that creates a change within the faith structure. For most of us, this would be the hoped for experience. For example, many people rely on worship and social support within a faith community. But, over a period of years, it may be that the very principles of faith being discussed and taught flourish within the inner recesses of one's heart. There is a longing for a more personally engaging faith. And a quest is begun for both the mystical presence promised in faith and the compassionate engagement of care for others in suffering. Faith takes root and new practices must be found to provide an adequate way of sustaining our faith quest. For some people, this faith quest will mean turning to retreats and classes in prayer. For others, it will mean totally disrupting their ordinary lives by embarking on mission trips and attending to the needs of the poor and suffering. Faith structure then must change as an expression of a growing faith. Can our faith community support us in these times of major change of focus as we express our quest for faith and meaning in new ways?

Breaking Out—Seeking a New Faith Structure

Is our faith adequate? Is our community of faith supportive of the stirrings of our hearts? Is our community of faith willing to wrestle with questions of faith as we are being inwardly pushed to do? It's very difficult for most people to have to say, "I must pursue new arenas of understanding."

Perhaps it is time to seek out a seminary or college religion class in order to think afresh about the nature of God. Perhaps we will find resources in local retreat centers or training programs in spiritual formation to discover new ways of practicing our faith. Bookstores are filled with volumes that can help us in both of these arenas. But, do we have a community for conversation that is open to the exploration of these concepts with us? Can we find a variety of ways of worshiping and relating within our faith community to enable our needed growth or is it a time to search out a new community of faith? Who will be our conversation partners to help renew a coherent sense of personal meaning? If God is no longer experienced through particular worship and prayer experiences, perhaps we need to break out and begin a search for new practices to renew our felt experience of God. Breaking out can be very confusing yet very rewarding.

Unstable Faith Structure

Finally, there may be times during which our faith structure is unstable, periods of time when we do not have a sustainable faith structure. Perhaps we have never had a relationship with a faith community or faith practices for any sustained period of time. We vaguely wonder if something is missing. Or perhaps we are in a kind of wilderness time when our spiritual essence and the way faith is practiced within our faith community are diverging. We have not yet ascertained how to deal with this difficulty, but we long for a better fit. Perhaps the disruption of faith life is actually the dynamic movement of God. A deep sense of disquiet is often the precursor of pending change. We must endure a sense of discomfort in our faith lives for a period of time. Perhaps we are in a time of major shifts in psychological self-understanding, waking from years of dependency on other people, and we are beginning to recognize the inadequacy of our understanding of God. We do not know what to do, but we know the old ways of relating to God are not working. We do not know how to proceed and we endure a sustained period of confusion. Perhaps it has never occurred to us that it is appropriate to "dust off" our concept of God from time to time. We've suddenly found ourselves longing for an adequate faith structure, knowing we have begun a time of profound reorientation to life itself. It's beginning to occur to us that our faith structure must remain in a confused state for a period of time, uncomfortable as it is to be in such unknown terrain.

As I write about these dynamics, I'm aware of a certain taboo that may exist for many of us around asking such probing questions regarding the practice of faith. Perhaps it is for this reason that so many of us hit a deep faith crisis, suddenly realizing that our faith is not our own, but the faith of our childhood. I'm clearly suggesting a different model, the model taught by Jesus to Nicodemus in the first great teaching story of the Gospel of John:

There was one of the Pharisees named Nicodemus,
a member of the Jewish Council, who came to Jesus by night.

"Rabbi," he said, "we know that you are a teacher sent by God;
no one could perform these signs of yours unless God were with him."

Jesus answered,
"In truth, in very truth I tell you, unless a [person] has been born over again,
[that one] cannot see the kingdom of God."

"But how is it possible," said Nicodemus,
"for a [person] to be born when . . . old?
Can [we] enter [our] mother's womb a second time and be born?"

Jesus answered,
"In truth I tell you, no one can enter the kingdom of God without being born
from water and spirit.
Flesh can give birth only to flesh;
it is spirit that gives birth to spirit.
You ought not to be astonished, then, when I tell you that
you must be born over again.

The wind blows where it wills;
you hear the sound of it, but you do not know where it comes from,
or where it is going.

So with everyone who is born from spirit."
—JOHN 3:1–8 (NEB)

This text has been interpreted far too often only one way, that of seeking the new birth, the "born again" experience of Christianity. This is one legitimate reading of the story. To limit the text to that one experience, however, does not do justice to the dynamism of the images. In the Greek New Testament, there is a single word that is translated in English by at least three words: spirit, wind, breath. That word is *pneuma*. So, when Jesus is telling Nicodemus that he must be born again, he is saying he must be born into the life of the Spirit. To dwell in the life of the Spirit is to be subject to its promptings, which are like wind. It seems to me it would be much more appropriate to translate the line "You must be born over again" as "You must be born over again . . . and again . . . and again . . . and again." That kind of ongoing creative change process is true to our life experience.

Life structure changes. Faith structure changes. Jesus calls us into the creative life with God as companion. To what new life is the Spirit now calling you? Listen to your deep disquiet and longings. They will guide you to the new life calling in the Spirit.

For the Discerner

In these exercises we will reflect on the themes of life structure and faith structure. After this exploration, we'll listen to our inner sighs and longings emerging for this time of discernment.

I. Life Structure/Faith Structure
- Think about your current life structure. Consider the following:
  - Describe your living situation:
    With whom are you living?
    Describe your home. Do you own or rent? Do you have pets?
    Describe your neighborhood. What are things you particularly like about it?
    Do you have people with whom you regularly interact—neighbors, friends, your auto mechanic, grocery checkout clerk, bank teller?
  - Describe your work life. How is your sense of satisfaction with your work? What do you most enjoy? What is problematic?
  - Describe your financial resources. Do you have a sense of financial stability or instability?
  - Describe your network of friends, work associates, and acquaintances? How adequate do you experience these different kinds of relationships?
  - What are your hobbies or leisure activities?
  - What else would you like to write down to locate your sense of life structure?
- Faith structure
  - Describe your relationship to a faith community.
  - Describe your use of faith practices (such as prayer, meditation, personal or group Bible study or other spiritual group, attendance at worship, community outreach activities).

- Briefly describe your understanding of God (use just a few words).
- Do you actively use symbols, practices, images from your faith to help you sort out issues of life meaning? How does this work for you? Give an example, if you can.
- What is your sense of your personal experience of God at this time?
• Previous life structure
  - Think of a specific time in the past, naming a time and the place where you were living, then describe your life structure at that time.
  - Use the same themes to describe your life structure as noted above.
• Previous faith structure
  - Describe your faith structure at that time using the themes previously noted.
• Life and Faith Changes
  - Compare your previous life and faith structures with your present ones. How have you changed? How has your faith life changed?
  - Now, reflect on the differences. You may be surprised at how much has changed. Such life circumstances change gradually.
  - What aspects of your faith structure have changed? Are you more or less content with your faith life now than at this time in the past?
  - In light of changes in your life structure and faith structure, reflect on Jesus' image of the new birth into Spirit. Read again a portion of the Scripture.

Jesus answered,
"In truth I tell you, no one can enter the kingdom of God
without being born
from water and spirit.
Flesh can give birth only to flesh;
it is spirit that gives birth to spirit.
You ought not to be astonished, then, when I tell you that
you must be born over again.

The wind blows where it wills;
you hear the sound of it, but you do not know where it comes from,
or where it is going.

So with everyone who is born from spirit."

— How is God's Spirit blowing as a gentle breeze in your life or in the lives of those close to you? What gentle changes is this Spirit inviting?

— Perhaps God's Spirit is blowing in your life as a major wind for change. Or in the lives of those near to you. What major changes is the Spirit inviting?

— What practices of faith do you need now to help you sort out the changes of life structure calling to you?

2. Inward Groanings/Deep Longings

After you have a sense of location within your life structure/faith structure, listen to your inward "groanings." Articulate more clearly the places of discontent stirring within you. How might the *pneuma* be stirring you to acknowledge areas of needed attention as you seek realignment of your life? Listen for your "sighs too deep for words" in three domains: personal, family or close relationships, and world/political issues.

Make three lists of your deepest concerns or your inward "sighs" (I've offered examples of such concerns):

Personal

1. listening for inspiration for next phase of life

2. _____

3. _____

Family and Relationships

1. fear for sons' safety as they go into world

2. _____

3. _____

World

1. overwhelmed by global disasters

2. _____

3. _____

For each concern, phrase a prayer request or turn this issue into a positive statement for action/implementation or positive affirmation.

Live with your prayers and affirmations for a week or more.

What insights have you gained that may contribute to your deeper questions of life calling?

3. Just for Fun

What is one thing you will do in the next few weeks, just for fun? This can be very simple, such as lunching with a friend, taking a walk, going to a movie.

Name it _____ Schedule it _____

4. Practicalities

What information gathering, budget planning, conferring with others, etc., do you need in light of these reflections?

Revisit your previous lists of practicalities. What needs to be done in the next few weeks? What goes into your information file?

Notes

1. Teilhard de Chardin to his cousin Marguerite Teilhard, July 4, 1915 in *The Making of a Mind*, 57–58.

2. Daniel J. Levinson with Charlotte N. Darrow, Edward B. Klein, Maria H. Levinson, Braxton McKee, *The Seasons of a Man's Life* (New York: Ballantine Books, 1978).

3. "Now hope that is seen is not hope. For who hopes for what is seen? But if we hope for what we do not see, we wait for it with patience" (Rom 8:24–25).

4

Weaving the Fabric of Community: Balancing Life with Others and Life Calling

You shall love the Lord your God with all your heart, and with all your soul, and with all your strength, and with all your mind; and your neighbor as yourself.
—LUKE 10:27

The hero/heroine's journey helps us to discover our life callings as individuals. Indeed, we might envision this hero/heroine's journey as it plays out over the cycles of our lives as a primary way that we continue to discover and express our uniqueness. Carl Jung wrote of the process of "individuation."[1] By the term, individuation, Jung meant the healthy human functioning that leads us into a process of unique self-differentiation, self-discovery, and self-expression. There is a dynamism to this process of individuation. If we do not seek out our sense of unique life calling, we will not find deep meaning in life. James Hillman has written of attending to the inner *daimon*, our sense of unique personal destiny. As we live the cycles of the hero/heroine's journey, we hope to grow more fully into our sense of inner calling. This inner calling, however, is not only about our personal achievements and unique path of service; it is also about our destiny within our families and our social networks. How is our *daimon*, our sense of life destiny, being played out with regard to marriage or other intimate partnership, deep friendships, children, and parents?

Balancing our sense of unique personal destiny are the tasks of relationships—the joys and difficulties we find in living with family, working with colleagues, and the meaning we find in serving others. Ernest Boyer Jr. wrote an intriguing description of the tasks of spiritual life.[2] In his book, he spoke of two kinds of spirituality: the spirituality of the center and the spirituality of the edge. He describes a powerful moment in a class he attended on the desert fathers and mothers of early Christianity. They found their spiritual calling by imitating Jesus, going into isolation in the desert regions of Palestine, Syria, and Egypt. Early monastic life developed from their experience. As a young parent with a deep sense of longing for this spiritual life and with profound frustration, he asked the instructor, "Is there childcare in the desert?"[3]

Boyer names one of the profound spiritual issues in our time. Most of us are not living the highly individualistic life of early hermits in the desert. We live in society, in communities, and in families. Yet, the resources from Christian spirituality largely reflect the individual quest for purity of soul before God. Even when engaging in a communal living situation, such as monastic life, our spiritual legacy of prayer and attention to the inner journey helps us primarily with the task of solitary communion with God. How do we make sense of the other great calling before us, life in community, in families, in corporate structures—in short, life in the world?

Boyer's response was to speak of two equally powerful and significant forms of spirituality. By the "spirituality of the center," he describes life in both the world and in the daily rhythms of family. Through living intentionally with the tasks of daily life with others, the "spirituality of the center" calls us to grow in the midst of commitments to other people, commitments that can last a lifetime. I would describe this attention to living creatively in community as "weaving the fabric of community." It is a very powerful theme within Scripture, as we'll see. Weaving the fabric of community provides the balance to the other form of spirituality described by Boyer, the "spirituality of the edge."

That edge spirituality is the one sought by the early Christian monastics. The principles of the spirituality of the edge are essential for us all. It is critical that we go to the edge of our society sometimes. It is very important to "retreat" from the demands of life to gain perspective. It is imperative that we seek God alone and have time alone with our own thoughts and concerns. The spirituality of the edge has given us practices of contemplative prayer and meditation. It is the spirituality of Christ summoning us one by one to pick up our cross and follow him. Yet, to what tasks does Christ summon us? Doesn't he ultimately call us back into the center of our society? Aren't we summoned to create communities of peace and justice? Aren't we individually called to care for the least among us? We must retreat in order to be clear about how to engage. Even in the individualistic hero/heroine's journey, the hero and heroine finally return to enrich the communal life they left behind by giving their discoveries as an elixir for others. The story of the heroic quest is not complete until that return has occurred and community life has been enhanced.

A significant part of my life story is that Ruth and I started our family in our early forties. Perhaps because I was an older parent, I may have been excessively focused on my career. While the daily tasks of caring for our infant sons were often overwhelming, they were oddly liberating. It was impossible for me to be self-focused. The daily tasks of parenthood were all consuming. The fabric of community our family was weaving together was no longer in service to abstract good causes, it was immediate and inescapable.

The rigors and rewards of the spiritual task of "life at the center" were a grand discovery for me. In the summer of 2008 we celebrated receiving our first daughter-in-law into our family. When I think of the absolute joy and love generated by this young couple in their wedding celebration, I think quite differently about what is truly important. Weaving the fabric of community, in which families merge, in which life is lived in company with one another through times of birth, achievement, disappointment, illness, new relationships, and our children's quest for vocational identity—these tasks become paramount. At times in our lives, our personal struggles for achievement are in the foreground. At other times, our life in family relationship is in the foreground. Both are critical. I find it strange that our primary understandings of spiritual life do not speak more directly of the power of these moments of great family celebration as times of divine epiphany—birth, marriage, and, often, funeral tributes to a life well lived.

In my experience, those are the deepest and most powerful experiences of divine presence. Mirroring the experience of great joy in our son and daughter-in-law's marriage celebration were the other great moments of such family gatherings for me—the deaths of my parents. The great outpouring of community support and love in each time of memorial was astounding. What a great privilege many of us have to mark such moments that are both so private and yet also so public. While few of us will experience all of these, when we have opportunity for such public/private times of community sharing, we are extremely blessed, brought face-to-face with the goodness of life well lived.

Here is a description of the rediscovery of the importance of a family time by a very busy man:

> I just took five days in Chicago with my family and what a trying, learning, and wonderful experience it was. I had scheduled a long overdue family vacation. With the price of gas so high, we decided to go to Chicago and dig up all we could do. We purchased a City-Pass which gave us access to the Field Museum, Shedd Aquarium, Adler Planetarium and Sears Tower. The first day was trying. Not realizing how much older my kids are (sixteen and thirteen), we were four in one hotel room and the challenges were many. The first night we bought a game called OUTBURST. In this game you try to get your teammate to say a word without you saying it. This was the highlight of the trip. We had always been a game playing family, sometimes eating a steak dinner with a SORRY! board in the middle of the table. This wonderful spirit of unity was quickly resurrected and our jail-cell like hotel room became the most anticipated place to be at the end of every day. More importantly, it did something for me spiritually. It reminded me of how great God is as I watch my babies become adults. It reminded me of love, sharing and a father's role of protecting his family. It was not about bottom lines and meeting deadlines; it was just about having fun and being with the ones I love most. And it felt good.[4]

Because of the power of this experience, this man set out to change the fundamentals of his work environment so he could spend more time with his family.

To balance the call to uniqueness embedded in the hero/heroine's journey, let us look to biblical stories focusing on weaving the fabric of community. Let's begin with the story of Joseph (Gen 37–50).

Joseph's story, while it can be told through the model of the hero/heroine's journey, is fundamentally the model story for weaving the fabric of community. Joseph is one of Jacob's sons, who, because of his brothers' jealousy, is sold into slavery to the Egyptians. It is intriguing that the symbol for Joseph is his "coat of many colors." *Fabric* is Joseph's symbol. This beautiful fabric is desecrated by Joseph's jealous brothers. But in Egypt, because of his integrity, his understanding of the interior world of dreams, and his administrative skill, Joseph is able to save the Egyptians, preserving them from famine, as well as being present to his family in their time of crisis. Through his personal capacity for forgiveness and his love for his father, brothers, and their families, he rescues them from famine and brings them to Egypt. Joseph uses all of his mature skills, gained in his years of exile, to rebuild the communal fabric for his own family.

It is that saving effort on Joseph's part that led to the people of Israel being in Egypt. Not only did he care for his own family but he also helps the people of Egypt. He provides stores of food for thousands of people during a time of famine. The social fabric of the Israelites, after their generations of intermingling, is unraveling under slavery. Here we take up the story of Moses, and the call of God to deliver the people out of Egypt. During the forty years of nomadic life in the desert, the Israelites regulate themselves according to the new law of the Ten Commandments and are sustained by manna, the unexpected physical bounty in the wilderness. Thus, Moses' story is also one of weaving the fabric of community. The Ten Commandments point to essential principles for communal life together (Ex 20).

The Ten Commandments place great emphasis on honoring—honoring God as well as father and mother. Honoring others is the foundation for life in community. When we honor God, when we have no other gods before God, it means that we are in a perpetual state of holding ourselves before "All that Is." Loving God with all of our hearts and souls and minds and strength means that we are devoting all of our life energies to God, who enfolds every human being, every social order, every plant, every animal, and every galaxy. To hold ourselves accountable before God is thus to affirm the communal fabric of life itself. Honoring God is also honoring our interconnections.

We are further enjoined to honor father and mother, as the symbol and practical exercise of holding ourselves accountable to the community that has formed and shaped us. We are thus trained to give fundamental respect to others by giving fundamental respect to our parents.

The Ten Commandments instruct us to maintain ourselves in right relationship to God and society by honoring the Sabbath, the one day per week we cease all of our self-directed activities and remember essentially who we are.

The other Ten Commandments point to fundamental human rights: the right to life ("Thou shalt not kill" [KJV]), to marriage ("Thou shalt not commit adultery"), to property ("Thou shalt not steal"), to honesty in public affairs ("Thou shalt not bear false witness"), to individuality ("Thou shalt not covet").[5] In other words, the communal fabric will be sustained if we approach it with respect for the individual. The individual will be sustained only through a supportive communal fabric. A society may be judged and held accountable on these principles.

Balancing the Solitary Journey with Weaving Communal Fabric

As we explore the great themes of Scripture we discover that the essence of Christian spirituality can be described as finding the balance between the "solitary" heroic journey and the tasks of "weaving the fabric of community." The first task takes us into uncharted realms of personal discovery and creativity before God. Through the solitary journey, God inspires us to reshape our communities, often calling us out of them into new understandings. We are then sometimes called back to offer our insights to our communities. The second task takes us into the struggle of living daily in community, honoring and respecting ties of family, friends, and coworkers, with whom we live out our callings. The spirituality of the solitary journey causes us to seek God before fulfilling even our family and social obligations. The spirituality of weaving the fabric of community causes us to seek God in the midst of relationships, responsibilities, and everyday life. Both are essential.

One of the struggles of our time is that, with the displacement of so many people from their communities of birth, we must consciously work at creating community wherever we live. At last count, I realized that I had lived in more than twenty houses in over sixty years. Many other people will have similar stories. This inordinate amount of change means that we need now more than ever to recognize that creating a sense of community is a spiritual practice.

Jesus' great teaching confronts us: "You shall love the Lord your God with all your heart, and with all your soul, and with all your strength, and with all your mind; and your neighbor as yourself" (Luke 10:27). Our communal task is to love our neighbors. Sometimes that means that we must first create the climate in which people, even next door to each other, become neighbors in relationship, as well as in proximity. About fifteen years ago, I moved to a small town after living for over forty years in highly urbanized environments. I was surprised to discover the quest for a community of support and quality sustenance is as necessary in rural and small town environments as it is in large cities. We begin at the most basic levels, everywhere, to build community spirit that will be sustaining.

An interview with Elise, in Gail Sheehy's *New Passages*, provides eloquent testimony to the power of being committed to reaching out to build good relationships each day. Elise, a woman in her sixties, once had a full career and family. On the other side of major health problems and the death of her husband, she has come to a place of deep clarity about the purpose of her life:

> My own vocabulary of intimacy has extended. It's like a root system spreading out. It's much more expansive. I've had this intense feeling of being available to many people—women and men—as friends and acquaintances. I'm not willing to let a day go by where my life hasn't been touched, or I haven't touched someone else's life. And I feel very confident about taking risks along with the consequences. When you're younger, you're so strung out with responsibilities, you become very protective of your emotional energy. You think it's finite. It isn't. There's no limit to your emotional availability.[6]

For some people, the tasks of weaving the communal fabric come naturally. They are able to reach out to people easily. For others, it takes some conscious effort to open our homes and our personal lives to build a community of friendship. For some families, it takes great effort to come together over distances for times of family celebration and remembrance. Through her recent health and grief struggles, Elise found a new life calling, focusing daily on the quality of relationships surrounding her. To put it very simply, we need one another. And our lives are immeasurably enriched when we share in the joys of fellowship together. At a time of life transition, it may be very important to ask, how am I enabled, and with whom, to weave the fabric of community?

For the Discerner

1. Honoring

"Honoring" as it is used in the Ten Commandments is an intriguing term. It does not mean "obey," it does not mean only "respect," nor does it simply mean "pray for," yet it has a very significant connotation for how we are to be in relationship with others. Honoring entails a sense of profound regard, just as Joseph showed his family in their need.

As you reflect on the emerging tasks that are coming to light for you in the hero/heroine's journey, think about family members, groups of people, communities of the "least," who are regularly in your prayers and on your heart? Make a list of these persons. With each listing, consider how you are being called to "honor" this person or group of people. Remember that the ways you honored them in the past may not be the best way to honor them now. How you honor your children when they are five years old is quite different than when they are twenty.

2. Adjusting the Hero/Heroine's Journey

How can we balance the tasks of unique inner calling with that of utter regard for social concerns? Refer to your notes on the hero/heroine's journey from chapter 2. Rewrite the story from the perspective of the contribution of this unique sense of personal calling to the common good. Does this attempt to balance the two dimensions in light of the tasks of weaving the communal fabric create a sense of creativity or does it bring conflicts to light?

3. A Letter from God

In chapter 2 one of the exercises was to write a letter to yourself from God, as you were being formed in the womb. Write another letter to yourself from God, describing your contributions to the good of your family, your community, and your world. How would God see the contributions you have made to weaving the fabric of community? What remains for you to accomplish in this domain?

4. Circles of Community

Think of your life as lived in a series of increasing circles of community beginning with immediate family, expanding to extended family, to close friends, to your neighborhood, to your professional community, to circles of social concern (including your arenas of charitable giving), and expanding to include the whole world. In each of these domains, note areas of connectivity working well for you and areas of potential relationship needing further development.

5. Concern for Others/Concern for Self

Which comes more naturally to you—concern for others or concern for your self? As you reflect on your present discernment questions, does seeking a balance between these two dimensions assist you? Or is it perhaps time to focus on one dimension over the other?

6. Practical Issues of Community

What practical issues arise, with regard to your discernment process, from this focus on your sense of community and attention to your loved ones? Are there some new considerations which you must address? Are there additional areas of practical consideration?

7. Spiritual Disciplines for Discernment

Revisit the spiritual and physical disciplines you began in chapter 1. Perhaps these patterns are working well for you. Perhaps you would like to adjust what you have planned. Remember "daily" can mean four to five times a week. If you've not been doing some of these, perhaps you tried to commit to too much. Engaging in the exercises of each chapter presents a lot of material to process. Perhaps doing the chapter exercises is all that is reasonable for you to do. Recast the notion of "disciplines" as "time for myself."

8. Just for Fun
What is one thing you will do in the next week or two, just for fun? This can be very simple, such as going to lunch with a friend, taking a walk, going to a movie.

Name it _____ Schedule it _____

9. Practicalities
What information gathering, budget planning, conferring with others, etc., will you do now with reference to your discernment?

Revisit your lists from previous chapters. What needs to be done in the next few weeks? What goes into your information file?

Notes

1. M.-L. von Franz, "The Process of Individuation," in *Man and His Symbols*, ed. Carl G. Jung (New York: Dell, 1968).

2. Ernest Boyer Jr., *A Way in the World: Family Life as Spiritual Discipline* (San Francisco: Harper & Row, 1984); paperback edition, *Finding God at Home: Family Life as Spiritual Discipline* (New York: HarperCollins, 1988).

3. Ibid. xi.

4. Virgil G. Woods, personal communication, August 2008.

5. Near the end of his life, my father, Marvin T. Judy, wrote a small monograph (unpublished) on the Ten Commandments. I am indebted to his themes of the positive dimension of each commandment stated here.

6. Gail Sheehy, *New Passages: Mapping Your Life across Time* (New York: Ballantine, 1995), 403.

5

Life Stages
and Transitions

Now in her midtwenties, Laura has been on a very clear path of professional development. She went directly from undergraduate school to a master's degree program that has prepared her for ministry. As she entered her final year of seminary, she completed requirements for ordination. Yet, she remained unclear about her next professional step. Should she further prepare herself with PhD studies? How would she balance this possibility with her husband's professional goals? Was she ready for pastoral leadership? As she considered these questions, she and her husband were surprised by her pregnancy. Suddenly, all of Laura's plans fell into place. They would return to their family's location in a small town in the Midwest. Her husband would have work in a family business, which he had not seriously considered before. Laura would have ample opportunity for a ministry placement full or part-time in this region. They would have family support for their life as new parents. Laura would put her PhD on hold.

Laura's story demonstrates the principles of discernment with which we have been working. Laura pursued her own career path with diligence, as had her husband. As Laura and her husband explored the many options for their next steps, the commitment to family suddenly helped everything fall into place for their next career moves. In their story, they have demonstrated the principles of effort and surrender. They pursued their career aspirations carefully. Further career development was a distinct possibility for Laura. But, the baby has changed her priorities and enabled her to open to new connections with her family and a move into pastoral leadership. Both Laura and her husband look forward to reclaiming life in a region of the country that they truly enjoy. The effort of career development has yielded into surrender to a larger (and surprising) whole.

Roger is in his late sixties. He and his wife, Pam, own a small business. They expend substantial effort to sustain the level of income needed to live decently. Often, Roger wishes for an easier path, but sees no way to change course. His commitment to his business means that he has to let go of hopes for retirement anytime soon. Faced with the fact that they cannot afford to retire at the customary age, Roger and Pam have discovered an alternative. They find great joy in spending time at a small lake cottage. Recently Pam has joined Roger (whose passion for photography has been lifelong) in a new shared hobby of taking pictures together. Their motto is "take retirement one day at a time" and "be alert for the next photo opportunity." They must practice a complicated kind of surrender into the realities of life in order to keep up the effort required to sustain the business, while simultaneously claiming the joy of photography and their weekend cottage life.

Effort or Surrender

Did you get to where you now are in your life primarily through effort or surrender? Frances Vaughan posed that question to me in 1980. As a young man in my mid thirties, it was immediately clear to me that I would answer—through effort! In short, I thought of myself as creating my own achievements. And while, indeed, I had worked very hard, I was also full of a youthful hubris that I could only recognize some years later. Now, as I look back upon the twists and turns of my career path, I can clearly see my surrenders at work to unseen forces and the fortunes of life circumstance, which were at least as significant as any effort I generated. Yes, effort at each major decision point has been necessary, but the final decision always has required some surrender on my part—a willingness to enter into an unknown arena. The answers have always involved undertaking tasks I would not have thought to pursue. Even our decision to move from Texas to California in 1980 for graduate studies came as a solution Ruth and I had not imagined until a number of nudges began to clarify this possibility. The decision came as a discovery within a time of deep unknowing. So, my obvious answer turns out only to be partially true.

Now, as I reflect on my major career choices, I would say that each one has been a balance between effort and surrender. The more I think about these major times of transition, I see that a fundamental surrender is required— that of living into the next stage of life—with changing family circumstances, changing physical energies, changing economic realities, and changing priorities. At the same time, intentionality is also required. Sometimes, it seems fierce intentionality and great tenacity are demanded. Sometimes doors seem to open once we set our intention toward the new direction. We need to adopt a posture of active seeking, active engagement, active searching, while holding on to the capacity to adapt as new opportunities open.

In the examples of Laura and Roger, the concepts of effort and surrender are complex. For Laura, the surrender to the inevitable changes of parenthood ironically helped her to surrender into her pastoral role rather than striving toward more professional preparation.

While Roger would love to slow down his business efforts, he must surrender the idea of formal retirement. Yet he is able to live into a posture of "being" at the lake cottage and make time for his photography and visits with friends. Fortunately, he still finds his actual work very satisfying. He and Pam have made space in their lives to embrace a portion of life others might find more fully in retirement—"listening to the songbirds, watching the seasons change, and dwelling with the Holy One."

Recall Charlene, Todd, and Jeff, from chapter 1, who each are making profound changes in midlife. Charlene, while not achieving strong recognition in her career, has turned her attention to more satisfying avocational pursuits and has found a satisfying blend of creative life and career. Todd, with whom we began, has begun a major shift of his career by letting go of his current position. Jeff has renewed his ministry by reclaiming his life as artist.

We see in these examples three different life stages at work. Laura and her husband are making that first full commitment to adulthood; in midlife Charlene, Todd, and Jeff each seek new directions. At the entry point to elder adulthood, Roger and Pam find they must make adjustments because of economic realities, yet still seek a balance within their life appropriate to their new life stage. Others are able to embrace retirement as an opportunity for a new life pattern. You may also recall Jim's difficulty in his early sixties in recognizing a calling away from his dominant mode of "doing" to a life focused in the perspective of "being." Living into each stage of life can be itself the cause of a major transition, as our interests and energies shift. The themes of effort and surrender will take on different nuances as our lives unfold over time.

Another way to describe the polarity of effort and surrender is in terms of the polarity of achievement and affiliation. Achievement directs us outward toward the world. It often engages us in fierce career undertakings. It can be highly competitive, requiring personal effort and discipline. We might describe the individual path of the hero/heroine's journey as the path of achievement. Affiliation is a psychological term for the tasks we have been describing as "weaving the fabric of community." Affiliation focuses on relationships and care for others. Affiliation helps us to make decisions based on the well-being of everyone concerned. Affiliation sometimes requires surrender of our own goals to best serve everyone else involved.

Life Stages Revised

We are the beneficiaries of almost five decades of helpful descriptions of the psychological processes associated with life stages. Erik Erikson's groundbreaking work, *Identity and the Life Cycle*, originally published in 1959, laid the foundation for psychologists and educators to think creatively about the changes that occur throughout life.[1] By the 1970s a new notion of adult life had begun to take hold of American culture. We began to think of adulthood not as a straight line of stability in one career from young adulthood to death. Instead, we began to think of cycles of adulthood, with periods of relative stability followed by times of instability leading to shifts and changes, followed by other periods of relative stability, and so on—cycles of our adult life story. We came to speak with acceptance of something called the midlife crisis, a time to reorient fundamental priorities. These researchers and writers gave us language for what Gail Sheehy calls the "predictable crises of adult life."[2] The popular discussion continued. A dozen years following the publication of *Passages*, Judith Viorst furthered these themes with her profound description of "necessary losses" as we progress through life.[3] In 1995, Gail Sheehy brought the popular discussion up to date with her book, *New Passages*.[4] Sheehy notes key components of early adulthood and the unique issues of the midlife decades: the forties, fifties, and sixties. She points toward developmental processes even later in life and notes particular themes, including medical issues, unique to women or to men. Her work in respect to gender issues reflects the scholarly discussion that has occurred noting the differences between men's and women's responses to adult life changes. In 1982, Carol Gilligan's *In a Different Voice* captured much of this discussion, critiquing the developmental theories so prevalent in Western psychology, which have lacked conversations with women about women's concerns.[5] Feminist writings in psychology and theology have profoundly altered the discussion of the role of women in society over these years.

A plethora of books on men's consciousness appeared in the 1990s, beginning with Robert Bly's *Iron John*.[6] Similarities and differences of women and men in brain structure, prompted by differences of hormonal impulse, are now part of our public discussion.[7] Even more recently, researchers are pointing to a fundamental change in the way of thinking that accompanies the shift into the sixties and seventies, what Gene Cohen has called the "mature" mind. This quality of mind seems more naturally balanced, integrating the needs of self and those of others and can even exhibit new qualities of creativity.[8]

Gail Sheehy notes that the clear demarcation of adult stages, thought to be normative thirty years ago, no longer holds up. In previous generations, twenty-year-olds were eager to flee their parents' home and make a place for themselves in the world of work and family. But, for economic reasons, many adult children are returning home after college or after other changes in their lives. In many cases couples delay child bearing into the forties or beyond. People may be forced into retirement earlier than they had anticipated. Others, like Roger, find ways to work a full schedule into their late sixties and seventies. Frequently, midlife women and men find a major career readjustment to be necessary. Health or financial reversals may derail an expected retirement. Even with these changes in predictable turning points of life, Sheehy describes major categories of adult life. She speaks of Provisional Adulthood from ages eighteen to thirty and First Adulthood from ages thirty to forty-five. She describes our Second Adulthood as beginning at age forty-five and often extending to eighty-five and beyond.

In Second Adulthood we enter the Age of Mastery. Sheehy describes the Age of Integrity beginning in the sixties and carrying onward.[9] More and more people are extending the Age of Integrity with very productive lives into the seventies, eighties, and nineties.[10] The number of centenarians continues to grow as well.

Rather than speaking of the Second Adulthood beginning in the mid-forties and continuing well into the eighties, some researchers make an even stronger demarcation regarding what Sheehy describes as the Age of Integrity. They speak of our life lived in quarters and describe the entry into the sixties as beginning the Third Quarter of life, reserving what was once called the aging process to the Fourth Quarter, when physical or mental debilitation may cause a radical change in our quality of life.[11]

For some people, early career choices have lasted for thirty or more years; for others there have been major career changes at each of the adult life stages. Similarly, when we have had children or when we have decided not to have children will mark critical junctures. For some people, there will be significant changes in intimate relationships as well, through marriage, divorce, or widowhood and perhaps remarriage.

As is readily apparent, when we map our own lives across time,[12] there will be unique patterns for each of us. Erikson's descriptions of life tasks, developed for particular life stages, are helpful for reflection at any stage of life. Erikson identifies eight such themes:

trust vs. mistrust

autonomy vs. shame/doubt

initiative vs. guilt

industry vs. inferiority

identity vs. identity diffusion

intimacy vs. isolation

generativity vs. self-absorption

integrity vs. disgust/despair[13]

While there are unique tasks in his formulation related to life stages, the themes are universal. For example, if we divorce or our spouse dies, we may well find ourselves revisiting themes of intimacy versus isolation. Even themes we thought were resolved in childhood may haunt us in times of major life upheaval.

In *The Life Cycle Completed*, Joan Erikson added a ninth stage,[14] old age. She makes the fascinating observation that because of the onset of debilitation, we may well revisit any of the previous eight life stages, but with the fragile perspective of dealing with the dystonic element as prominent. That would be the right side of any of these polarities. So, for example, despair may well arise even after a lifetime of achievements. Identity confusion may arise with changes of life circumstances. Joan Erikson has given us a profound window into the fragility of this very difficult period of life. It is a rare privilege for many of us who work in spiritual direction or in our visitation with elder friends and family to listen to their life stories and help them claim their achievements. During the diminishments of our physical or mental capacities, we need companions for prayer and for support in prayer even when our own capacities for prayer may be waning.

Achievement vs. Affiliation

One of the most comprehensive discussions of lifelong development is offered by Jenny Wade in her book, *Changes of Mind*.[15] She draws on psychological theories and on theories of consciousness, including consciousness in the afterlife, to discuss lifelong "changes of mind" that occur within us.

The following diagram is adapted from *Changes of Mind* by Jenny Wade.[16]

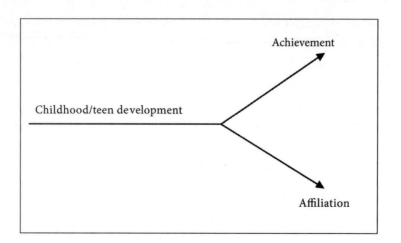

Based on her analysis of many psychological theorists, Wade shows that as we enter adult life, we typically find ourselves making decisions based primarily on the polarity between "achievement" and "affiliation." Achievement is the drive toward power and personal autonomy. Affiliation is seeking community, mutuality, and commitment to people. An intriguing thing happens, however, as we journey through adulthood. Whichever pathway has not been dominant begins to emerge. An achiever must learn to seek affiliation. Life requires such a balance from us. Wade completes the diagram by showing a radical reorientation that occurs for healthy individuals in later life:[17]

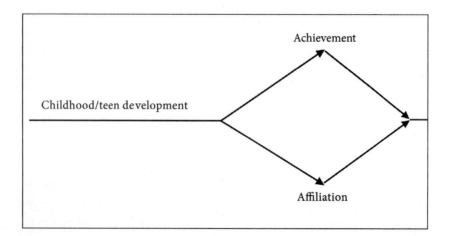

For example, when our sons were born, I had to balance achievement with the tasks of daily care of two young children. It was actually a relief for me, in a way that I had not expected, to have my focus balanced this way. Affiliation took place in a new and very immediate way. For me, this balance was very important. I can only wonder if I would have found such a balance between achievement and affiliation if we had not had children when we did.

As I have shared this model, many people have found it to be extremely helpful in seeking to understand the shifts taking place in their fundamental orientation to life. For a woman who has always made her decisions based first upon family concerns, even if she has also been in the workplace, there may come a time when she must attend to her own unique calling, independent of any other concerns. Care for others does not fall away, but a time has come for it to take second place in her quest for her unique calling before God. Or a woman who has early been on a high achievement track in her career may face the question of interrelationships with family and spouse in new ways.

Many men will experience this issue in a stark way. Many, like me, have been so focused on achievement in their careers that relationship, even with a beloved wife, has clearly been secondary. It took years of gentle and not so gentle confrontation with Ruth for me to understand what genuine mutuality in our marriage and decision process would look like. Many marriages falter because the partners are not able to shift from basic life stances on affiliation and achievement issues. Each is literally blind to the other way of thinking and being. Additionally, the arrival of children becomes another make-or-break point of decision. Will both spouses be able to devote adequate time to achievement pathways, while devoting essential energy toward affiliation needs for their children? Many families with young children struggle with these questions.

In recent years, as I've discussed these dynamics in retreats and classes, I've discovered I'm as apt to find women who took the high achievement role early in life as those who took the more expected affiliative role. Similarly, in some families, the man may be the primary caregiver attending to the affiliation/psychological needs of the family while the woman engages in career development. Gender roles are changing. Family constellations are changing. Single parenting is an astonishingly demanding path, requiring work outside the home as well as the nurture of children. Because of various family considerations, parents may put aside their own achievement needs while tending their children. But, after years of many small concessions, we may find our vocational dreams very diminished.

Balancing achievement and affiliation may be quite difficult for us. Some readers will have made major moves over their life spans due to following career choices. For others there has been great continuity of place and relationships and perhaps career choices have been secondary. Because of career moves, Ruth and I have suffered in the affiliative domain. Our deep friendships are with people in several different localities—a not uncommon situation of our time. The "world" seems to need many of us to be about a more national, even global, sense of loyalty in our vocational lives. As a friend once related to me, "I have wonderful friends all over the world, but it sure would be nice to have one close enough to have a cup of coffee together." May we each find a balance between deep relationships and meaningful careers. And throughout all, may our inward eyes continue to be illumined and our trust in God awakened.

For the Discerner

1. The way of Effort or Surrender
   Which way has dominated in your life decisions? Is one way more important to you in family life and another in your life in the world? How does your image of God affect these questions?

2. The Way of Achievement or Affiliation
   Which predominates for you in a major decision process—your commitments to your work and career or your commitments to family and friends? Are these two commitments a source of tension for you? How do you and your spouse, if you are married, deal with these issues? Are these sources of conflict between the two of you?

3. Life-Stage Issues
   Continue your reflection on your present life decision by being attentive to the following list of issues that reflects Erikson's life-stage issues.

Find one or two that particularly speak to you. Begin by noticing which of these words attract your attention, either by being an admirable attribute or one that troubles you:

- Trust
- Autonomy
- Ego Identity
- Intimacy
- Generativity
- Integrity
- Initiative
- Industry

- Mistrust
- Shame/Doubt
- Identity Confusion
- Isolation
- Stagnation (Self-Absorption)
- Despair
- Guilt
- Inferiority

For each of these significant words:

— Journal your associations with the word.
— Journal your past with that word.
— Journal your future aspirations for claiming or moving beyond the connotations of that word.

4. Just for Fun

What is one thing you will do this week or next, just for fun? This can be very simple, such as going to lunch with a friend, taking a walk, going to a movie.

Name it _____ Schedule it _____

5. Practicalities

What information gathering, budget planning, conferring with others, etc., will you do in the next few weeks with reference to your discernment?

Revisit your lists from previous chapters. What needs to be done now? What goes into your information file?

Notes

1. Erik H. Erikson, *Identity and the Life Cycle* (New York: Norton, 1980); see also Erik H. Erikson, *Life Cycle Completed: Extended Version with New Chapters on the Ninth Stage of Development by Joan M. Erikson* (New York: Norton, 1997).

2. Gail Sheehy, *Passages: Predictable Crises of Adult Life* (New York: Dutton, 1974, 1976).

3. Judith Viorst, *Necessary Losses: The Loves, Illusions, Dependencies, and Impossible Expectations That All of Us Have to Give Up in Order to Grow* (New York: Fireside, 1998).

4. Gail Sheehy, *New Passages: Mapping Your Life across Time* (New York: Ballantine, 1995).

5. Carol Gilligan, *In a Different Voice: Psychological Theory and Women's Development* (Cambridge, MA: Harvard University Press, 1993).

6. Robert Bly, *Iron John: A Book about Men* (Reading, MA: Addison-Wesley, 1990).

7. Deborah Blum, *Sex on the Brain: The Biological Differences between Men and Women* (New York: Penguin Putnam, 1997).

8. Gene D. Cohen, *The Mature Mind: The Positive Power of the Aging Brain* (New York: Basic Books, 2006). See also, Zalman Schachter-Shalomi and Ronald S. Miller, *From Age-ing to Sage-ing: A Profound New Vision of Growing Older* (New York: Warner Books, 1995).

9. Sheehy, *New Passages*, 9–10.

10. Ibid., see contents, xix–xxv, and prologue, 3–20.

11. "Counseling for the Third Quarter of Life," ed. Richard Haid and Caitlin Williams, special issue, *Career Planning and Adult Development Journal* (San Jose, CA: Career Planning and Adult Development Network) 15, no. 3 (fall 1999).

12. The subtitle of *New Passages* is *Mapping Your Life across Time.*

13. Erikson, *Identity and the Life Cycle*, 129.

14. Erikson, *The Life Cycle Completed*, 106.

15. Jenny Wade, *Changes of Mind: A Holonomic Theory of the Evolution of Consciousness* (Albany, NY: State University of New York Press, 1996).

16. Ibid., 134.

17. Diagram adapted from Wade, *Changes of Mind*, 158.

6

Passionate Commitment and Creative Relinquishment

Very truly, I tell you, unless a grain of wheat falls into the earth and dies,
it remains just a single grain; but if it dies, it bears much fruit.
—JN 12:24

Seasons of Living/Seasons of Change

One of the most challenging themes for persons living in concert with the creativity of God is how to attend to present passions while releasing those tasks that are complete. Instead of being in a flow of engagement and release, of attachment and detachment, of commitment and relinquishment, we tend to live as emotional houses, accumulating too much stuff in our basements or attics. We cling to the past, continuing to serve those passions of yesterday, while neglecting to make adequate space in our hearts for the next season of life and service. As we listen for initiatives emerging in our lives by God's creative summons, we need to ask, "What must I release, in order to make way for that which is calling now?" Or to return to our progenitors of faithful living, Abraham and Sarah, "What am I being asked to leave behind as I set off on God's new adventure?" It can be quite difficult for us to make such changes, even when we know how essential it is to let go of some of our life patterns and commitments. Certain aspects of our previous life structure may not serve us as we move into the next phase of life.

As Ecclesiastes 3:1 declares: "For everything there is a season, and a time for every matter under heaven. . . ." We can be helped in the task of letting go by thinking of the seasons of the year. The seasons naturally lead to growth, harvest, and fallowness. As we review the tasks of our present life transition, we need to attend to autumn, letting go of old patterns that have reached fruition, while embracing the necessary loss of winter and awaiting the new life of springtime.

Let's rejoin Jim in some of his considerations as he moves toward retirement. It is four years after the experience in Colorado recorded in chapter 3, in which Jim spoke of the possibility of a life more geared to "being" than to "doing." Because of his contract position in the university, Jim has certain skills in consulting that he will continue to use part-time as his primary work after retirement. He has also noticed that "being" is becoming important to him. When he is on breaks from his full-time job, he relishes working about half-time and devoting the other part of his time to simple tasks like gardening and doing odd jobs around his house. A plan is beginning to emerge as he tries to listen to where his spirit is most engaged in life issues and where certain work tasks have become boring and repetitive. The major loss he expects is in an upcoming move. Jim was divorced twenty years ago; he remarried fifteen years ago. Between them, he and his wife have four adult children and three grandchildren in their blended family. They plan to move to another state near two of their adult children and their families. Jim remains hopeful that the real estate market will cooperate by his planned date for retirement in two years.

Jim's anticipated move requires a major loss because he has greatly enjoyed the home in which he has lived for the past fifteen years. He has been deeply nurtured by this particular physical environment. When work or personal pressures have been intense, he has only needed to come home to find renewal. But, as this phase of life ends, he knows he must choose a new life in which he and his wife can make new friends, support their children's families, and create new patterns of community engagement. If he is to be vitally engaged in the next phase of life, this particular grain of wheat must fall to the ground and die. He must let go of something quite dear to him and literally move on in order to claim the gifts that await in the new environment.

The seasonal nature of life and calling is dramatically described for us by Jesus:

I am the real vine, and my Father is the gardener.
Every barren branch of mine he cuts away;
and every fruiting branch he cleans, to make it more fruitful still.
You have already been cleansed by the word that I spoke to you.
Dwell in me, as I in you.
No branch can bear fruit by itself, but only if it remains united with the vine;
no more can you bear fruit, unless you remain united with me.
I am the vine, and you the branches.
[Those] who [dwell] in me, as I dwell in [them], [bear] much fruit;
for apart from me you can do nothing.
[Those] who [do] not dwell in me [are] thrown away like a withered branch.
The withered branches are heaped together, thrown on the fire, and burnt.
If you dwell in me, and my words dwell in you,
ask what you will, and you shall have it.
This is my Father's glory, that you may bear fruit in plenty
and so be my disciples.
As the Father has loved me, so I have loved you.
Dwell in my love.
If you heed my commands, you will dwell in my love,
As I have heeded my Father's commands and dwell in his love.
I have spoken thus to you, so that my joy may be in you,
and your joy complete.
JOHN 15: 1–11 (NEB)

The growth, fruiting, and decline appearing through the seasons is the framework of this powerful statement describing life with Christ. Our lives are described as branches of Christ, the living vine. We have seasons of growth and productivity. Then, the branches wither and die. Fruit that is a gift to the world is produced through a "flow" of divine expression into us. Without that sense of life-giving flow, we cease to produce such fruit. In this Scripture we can describe our lives as a series of seasons. We experience seasons of preparation, growth, harvest, then a period of fallowness, perhaps even the dying of that branch. When the time has come, are we ready to let go of a task that once was life giving to us and to the world? Is there a place in our life journeys for that fire to complete the fall season, burning leaves and dead branches with appreciation and joy? Or are we continuously propping up the old tasks, the old ways of being rather than allowing seasons of change to occur?

Creative Growth/Creative Relinquishment

A colleague and I began a conversation several years ago about changes in life purpose and adjustments to the seasons of life. We came up with the term "creative relinquishment" to describe the necessary laying aside of completed tasks. Can we make space for the new life toward which Christ calls us? Or are we too busy with yesterday's commitments to make room for the new mission emerging? Sometimes it is necessary to let go consciously, to relinquish a certain way of being in order to make space on our calendars and in our hearts to nourish the new life seeking to be born within us. It can be very hard to name these roles and determine which have come to fruition and which are still life-giving.

This Scripture lends itself to asking four questions of our life process at any given time:

1. What is growing well and producing fruit?
2. What is growing well but could use pruning?
3. What is "dead" wood?
4. What is ready to "sprout"?

As in our work with the hero/heroine's journey, the various domains of our life may present conflicts as we deal with these questions of growth. Our work with this Scripture will help us attend to the new life emerging, as well as our areas of continuing growth and those functions that have ceased to have life-giving energy for us.

For the Discerner

Our kaleidoscopic adventure in discernment is perhaps becoming a little perplexing for both discerner and spiritual director. Because of the complexity of our decision process, some issues may be clarifying while other aspects of our discernment are most likely very unclear. Karen wrote of such a time in her discernment process:

> Many of my journal entries have been about trying to discern God's will for my life. One day when I was praying I received a word picture that illustrates and describes how I feel. I see myself standing in what looks like a desert sandstorm and I am only able to stand and look forward. I am not able to see clearly and the sand stings my face as it blows against me. I can't go forward because I don't know where to step. But after awhile the sandstorm is not as strong and as I try to step forward I believe I might see a clearing beginning to occur.

Before we go further with other turns of the kaleidoscope for discernment and work with the themes of John 15, let's take stock. I ask the discerner as well as the spiritual director to help assess where the discerner is now in the core-decision process. Let's return to the key themes of chapter 1:

1. Reviewing Discernment Themes

   Take some time and consider these core questions. Review your writings and reflections to date in your discernment work. See which exercises point toward resolution. Then write out responses to the following questions:

   - What theme or themes do you bring to this process of discernment? What is becoming clear for you? What areas remain unclear?
   - What details would be necessary to know now in order to discern the outcome?
   - What are financial implications?
   - What are implications for family members or others close to you?
   - What kinds of decisions would you need from your employer in order to approach these issues clearly?
   - What image or images would describe your present emotional and spiritual relationship to this discernment issue? Can you make a drawing or find another kind of picture or physical representation of this image?
   - Are there key Scriptures or other wisdom sayings that are emerging for you as helpful to your discernment?

Now, reflect on these issues with the help of the kaleidoscopic perspective with which we began our discernment process in the foreword. It may be helpful to again think on the interlocking and sometimes conflicting aspects of this kaleidoscope of life forces.

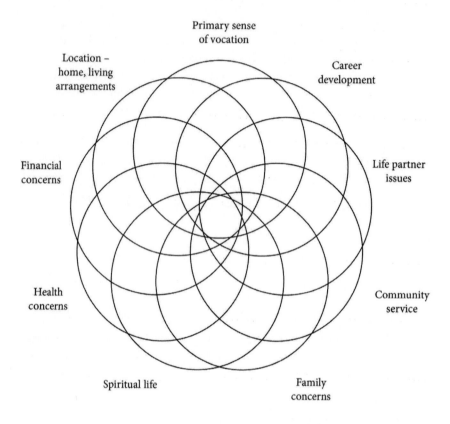

Primary sense
of vocation

Location –
home, living
arrangements

Career
development

Financial
concerns

Life partner
issues

Health
concerns

Community
service

Spiritual life

Family
concerns

As you discern, invite your spiritual director to review these things with you, inquiring about conflicts between areas or issues of loss that need to be acknowledged in your current life transition. Add these themes to your list of key issues and concerns. Ask how Scripture resources might help you in praying for clarity about these conflicts. If these reflections are taking place within a small group, be sure to take adequate time for each person to complete this process before moving on into reflections in the remainder of this chapter. Because of time constraints in your small group, you might do this exercise with one or two other persons and then make space for some general group reflection.

With this understanding of what is becoming clear about the discernment process, let's move onward to look more fully at our emerging passion and those areas of letting go that we must face.

2. Vine and Branches

Set aside an hour for this reflection.

As you have reflected on the major discernment themes in the first exercise, pick the primary theme that is emerging for your discernment, for example, location, career, or relationship. Or you may use this exercise as a general life structure review.

When you have named a domain for reflection, enter into the Scripture John 15:1–11 with an open heart. Spend some time becoming still. Read through it two or three times. Reflect on the profound invitation of Jesus to dwell with him and discover his indwelling within you. Dwell in his love. From that source of divine peace, then let yourself turn to the four questions:

• What is growing well and producing good fruit?

List areas that are going well, within the particular domain of your exploration or as a general life review. Be generous with yourself. List the activities and life tasks in which you feel fulfillment. If you are so inclined begin to draw a picture of the vine, noting roots for yourself. Your picture is only for your eyes. You can use different colors for different themes. Draw roots and branches, color in some clusters of grapes, or write words on your picture that describe these areas of fruitful living.

Take a little break and then turn to the next question:

• What is growing well but could use pruning (attention) to be more fruitful?

In the image of the grape vine, we have the description of God as the gardener. From time to time, God is going to prune off branches. Can we actively participate in such pruning? In this case, the main branch is remaining, but we can ask what areas would do better, would be more fruitful, if they were given more attention? We are working in the arena of metaphor and realities of life. For example, in order to grow in your spiritual life, do you need to devote more time to prayer and Bible study? What do you need to give up in order make the time for those tasks? Perhaps you begin to sense some shifting priorities in your family responsibilities. Perhaps this is a time of major care for aging parents. Would you be more effective if you were to release some other responsibilities for a year or two in order to be attentive to them? Continue to work with your lists and your drawings, returning to the Scripture if you feel that you've come to a conclusion with this kind of reflection. Perhaps you find some fresh inspiration from the Scripture, or perhaps you simply return to that sense of dwelling within Christ's love for a few moments.

Now is a great time to get a little refreshment, refill your tea or coffee, take a little walk outside or around the house. Then, turn to the hard question:

- What is "dead" wood?

   What is no longer growing? What activities are no longer life-giving to us but have become merely habits? What attitudes have become hindrances? Usually there are encrusted attitudes that need to be addressed. We have grown "hard" of heart in one or more ways. This part of the exercise can address attitudes and habits of mind or activity that have outlived their usefulness. You are not alone. We all go through such times of difficulty in letting go. This is the arena in particular to practice "creative relinquishment." What activities and attitudes need to be tossed into the bonfire for release? Making a bonfire of things it is time to release can be quite a profound exercise for us.

Again, take a little stretch and then turn to the question:

- What is ready to "sprout"?

   All of earthly life grows through seasons of renewal. Whether we speak of the plant or animal realms, life is perpetually renewing itself. What in your life is ready to be born? What new way of being or new tasks of doing are just about ready to emerge? What kind of space do they need in order to flourish? Note those areas on your vine. Are they completely new branches? Or do some of these new tasks grow out of existing branches? Be playful.

- Write an action plan.

  If you have time now, or perhaps in a day or two, review all that you've done with this exercise and then write an action plan for implementation. What needs to happen in order to make space for the new sprouting? What kind of attention do you need to give in a sustained way to those items you've identified for pruning? Do you need to make some hard choices among areas that are now going well and are fruitful in order to make some space for the new to emerge? How will you actually let go of the issues, attitudes, and activities you've identified for the burning pile? Do any of these in particular need sustained prayer? What themes do you need to bring to your spiritual director or a trusted friend for conversation? If you are working with a small group, identify one or two general themes from the exercise that you are comfortable sharing with your group members and identify any particular ways you would like to ask their assistance in helping you monitor your change process.

3. Just for Fun

   What is one thing you will do in the next week or two, just for fun? This can be very simple, such as going to lunch, taking a walk, going to a movie.

   Name it _____ Schedule it _____

4. Practicalities

   What information gathering, budget planning, conferring with others, etc., will you do now with reference to your discernment?

   Refer to previous lists. What do you need to accomplish now?

7

Revisiting the Call to Adventure

And God, who searches the heart, knows what is the mind of the Spirit, because the Spirit intercedes for the saints according to the will of God.

—ROM 8:27

In this chapter, I would like to amplify the themes of the hero/heroine's journey, introduce additional insights from Scripture, and offer an invitation to contemplate the call to adventure with attention to our relationship to God. Here, again, is the basic model.[1]

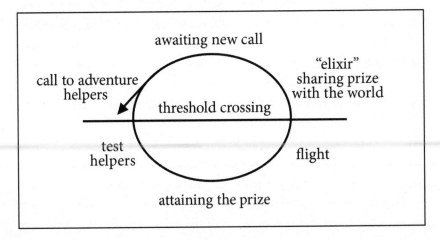

The Solitary Journey and the Quest for God

Let us explore in more detail the spirituality of the solitary journey. We have already discussed how it describes the calls of Abraham and Jacob. In the case of Abraham, a challenge is given by God along with a promise. It is the call to leave what is known and to venture into the unknown. This clarion call is one of the most familiar forms of spiritual call in our time. Particularly as people hit midlife, many have understood their call from God to be toward "change," often beginning a venture toward an unknown outcome. This call may convict some discerners to end a marriage or to release the comfortable and familiar in their life to embark on a new period of study. This call, like Abraham's, may literally have come as a summons to go to a new place. Frequently, the call to adventure comes through upheavals, such as a health crisis, a loss of work, or the death of a loved one. In recent years, many people have been thrust into a new call to adventure by the severe economic crisis. In all cases, the call to adventure can become a quest for authenticity before God.

The result of this quest can be the discovery of a new spirituality. Not infrequently, the quest for individual authenticity before God has called people to move beyond the boundaries of an earlier understanding of faith. One of the aspects of Campbell's description of the hero/heroine's journey is that it is a deeply spiritual quest.

Underneath the obvious quest for clarification of a vocation or a relationship is a deep quest for a new relationship with God. In the stories Campbell discusses from Scripture and mythology, the prize of the journey is also described in terms of relationship to God. He names these relationships with God in terms of three major categories: atonement, sacred marriage, or apotheosis.[2]

In the quest of atonement—making peace with a great call beyond oneself—are we not making peace with God who calls us to greatness? Atonement takes many forms. It is "at-one-ment" with God's call to search for a broader meaning for our lives. It is making peace with God, who calls us to do more than we think possible. Atonement is also illustrated by the sense of personal sacrifice required by such a commitment.

Could the search for God be termed a quest for sacred marriage? In its most classic form, sacred marriage is the union of a human being with the opposite-gender image of God. One of the most enduring forms of sacred marriage in Christian tradition has been the vow of marriage between women in religious orders and Christ. In goddess traditions, the sacred marriage was frequently understood as the union of the male youth with a goddess figure. In our time, sacred marriage appears in many ways. A fairy tale such as Sleeping Beauty describes the prince awakening the princess from slumber or from a state of unconsciousness. Marriage brings both persons into new life. In the Holy Grail stories, Gawain is on the search for his true love.[3] To find her is his grail quest. We can see sacred marriage as the dominant theme in the story of Jacob and Rachel. Jacob endures many labors in order to claim his true beloved (Gen 29). Sacred marriage is the underlying theme of romantic comedies in our movies.

Sacred marriage is quite prominent as people seek a life partner, divorce when disappointed, or seek another life partner. The sacred marriage may reemerge for couples in later life, as retirement puts them in much closer proximity. Our deep partner relationship may be the most significant force for spiritual awakening in our life. The spirituality of many people can also be described as union with God, not unlike that of the partnership of marriage. The inner union of an individual with God is a pervasive image in spiritual life. It can be experienced with profoundly deep emotional, even erotic, energies toward God as beloved.[4] That, too, is a sacred marriage image.

There is another kind of union with God, which Campbell describes as apotheosis, becoming one with God, a profound sense of union of human and divine. This kind of spiritual quest is described less frequently in Christianity than in some forms of Eastern religions. Yet, when we speak of being aligned with the Holy Spirit, when we speak in Christianity of inspiration of the Holy Spirit, these are union experiences.

In a couple's group that Ruth and I joined just after our sons were born, one of the older men was very clear that he had recently entered a quest for this kind of deep union with God. A direct experience of God was what was most important to him. He had entered a spiritual quest for apotheosis, becoming fully one with God. All else was secondary to him, even his relationships with family members and other people. I could only scratch my head at the time, as we were so involved in the mundane aspects of family life. With two infant children, my life was surrounded by diapers, crying, and intense personal care for these young lives. I was not focused on making a deeper union with God, except through fulfilling the obligations of parenthood. My life task at that time may perhaps be best described as atonement, making sense and coming to peace with the new challenges of fatherhood. Now, however, this man's focus makes much more sense to me, as I approach retirement and I hear Nancy's beautiful statement of her calling, as she affirms her desire to retire from her role in ministry supervision, to "watch the seasons, listen for the birdsongs, and dwell with the Holy One." Nancy shows me what apotheosis with God might mean in a way that speaks very deeply to me.

In chapter 5, I introduced a variety of themes related to faith structure. Let's return to those themes and look at them in light of the question for the discerner, "What kind of relationship with God are you currently seeking?" I described five dynamics of our relationship with God: (1) intellectual construct of God, (2) practices of faith, (3) relationship to faith community, (4) coherent sense of personal meaning, and (5) felt sense of God.

One of the exercises in this chapter will explore our relationship with God through these perspectives. What we gain from studying the hero/heroine's journey is a sense of the way God continues to surprise us throughout our life journey. A different form of relationship with God reveals itself from season to season in our lives. How would we describe our current sense of relationship with God? How might the five factors be changing during this time of life transition?

The following diagram shows the quality of interaction among the different themes. Think of the diagram as dynamic—the various themes pulsing with life-giving energy. Some areas will be richer and more life-giving at a particular time of life than others. We will seek to enliven all of these dynamics as part of the current discernment process.

The factors intersect with each other in a dynamic way. Any one of them can change at a given time of our life. Often, we will find major changes in several of them during times of transition. As a part of our discernment, it can be very helpful to review these essential characteristics of a faith life. Is our relationship with a faith community vital or do we need to renew our commitments or find a new faith community? Do our faith

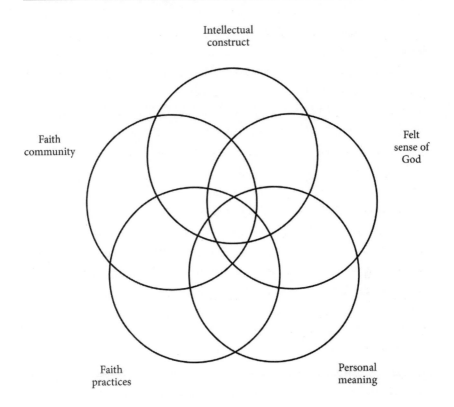

Intellectual
construct

Felt
sense of
God

Faith
community

Faith
practices

Personal
meaning

practices lead to a sustaining sense of God's presence? Does God seem absent from our present life struggles? Does our sense of understanding of God intellectually match our experience? Do all of these dynamics cooperate to produce a sense of personal meaning for our life? We would hope for the divine presence to energize our life decisions and to move us forward in our life transition. In this time of change, it would not be unexpected for many of these areas of faith life to be shifting. For some people, discovering a new way to practice faith will be the primary focus of the present quest for new life.

In Scripture, the solitary journey takes many forms. It can be the call to leave, to set out from the familiar, as it was for Abraham. It can be the confrontation to us of wilderness. Jacob received what he thought he wanted when he stole his brother's birthright. But as soon as he had attained this birthright, he found himself banished from his homeland. Then he fled into the wilderness. For us as well, the unexpected turns of life can initiate the solitary journey, through the sudden loss of loved ones or, as in Jacob's story, the feeling of emptiness after the achievement of a long-sought goal.

A very clear kind of wilderness experience described in Scripture is the spiritual struggle brought on by bereavement. The stories of Job and Ruth illustrate these terrible difficulties. For many people in our time, critical illness brings a similar disruption. Can we view our illness as a time of spiritual awakening to a new understanding of self and God?

Parenthood is a profound call for Sarah and for Mary and Joseph. Birth often comes as a surprising call from God to a whole new relationship with life as it shows us the indomitable power of God to unexpectedly bring new creation into the world. Elizabeth, who was considered barren, is pregnant with John. As the angel announces this to Mary, the proclamation is made: "For nothing will be impossible with God" (Luke 1:37). As we explore our present call to adventure, a wonderful way to ask what is happening is to phrase the question, "What is God trying to birth through me now?"

In these times of personal calling before God, we find God and self anew. We discover a new capacity for depth of relating to God, a new clarity about that which is just and unjust within our society, and a new awareness of the mystery of life itself. We can discover within ourselves wellsprings of divine love and hope for our society.

Weaving the Fabric of Community

The solitary journey and the quest for God leads us back to society with renewed vigor. But, beyond that, there is a unique task of spiritual life, which also requires ongoing attention under divine guidance—the task of sharing life in community. Ruth makes the choice within her bereavement for companionship. She and her sister Orpah make their spiritual choices based on which community they will choose for support in their new life without husbands. We may also, just as self-consciously, choose communities with which to live. There are special skills involved in holding ourselves accountable for God's action within the life of a community. For some, as for Jim, whose story we have been reviewing as he approaches retirement, a primary part of his current life transition is the search for clarity about where to live. This decision frequently occurs for people entering retirement, just as it does for young adults as they are beginning their first careers.

In working on this question, Jim and his wife are looking for a community near two of their adult children that can provide a strong social network, a place in which there will be opportunity for friendships, the stimulus of cultural events, and opportunities for meaningful service. As part of the discernment process is there a particular place that is calling us? Making such a choice based on place or a particular sense of community is a kind of quest often undertaken in Scripture.

How does our personal quest for life purpose relate to the health of the world community? That is a very big question, isn't it? Yet, that takes us back to the hope for our lives found in Romans:

> We know that the whole creation has been groaning in labor pains until now; and not only the creation, but we ourselves, who have the first fruits of the Spirit, groan inwardly while we wait for adoption, the redemption of our bodies. For in hope we were saved. Now hope that is seen is not hope. For who hopes for what is seen? But if we hope for what we do not see, we wait for it with patience.
>
> Likewise the Spirit helps us in our weakness; for we do not know how to pray as we ought, but that very Spirit intercedes with sighs too deep for words. And God, who searches the heart, knows what is the mind of the Spirit, because the Spirit intercedes for the saints according to the will of God.
>
> —ROM 8:22–27

As we explore the deep calling of our lives, may we be filled with hope for the peace, justice, and ecological wholeness of all peoples of the earth. May we struggle with the way our sense of personal life calling relates to this sense of hope for all people, across the street, around town, and all over the world. To struggle with such hope brings us face-to-face with our sense of life meaning. Do we somehow see our unique and very small circle of influence related to the grand hope of God for all creation? We remain unsatisfied unless we can make those essential links between our own lives and the greater life of the world.

In his profound statement, Paul helps us discover God's voice. As we listen to the inward groanings of our own spirits for peace, justice, and loving relationships within our families, our communities, and our world, we are actually participating in God's hopes. The Holy Spirit is showing us how to pray. We are being asked to participate in God's grand hope for the world. So, as we think about our own personal callings at this phase of life, we need to review our responses to the needs of the world. We may need to reassess our charitable giving. Are our donations congruent with the inner callings of God within our hearts? Perhaps we need to reassess the use of our volunteer time. Is the hope stirring in our hearts for the health of the world calling us to make a major career shift? Attention to weaving the fabric of community can provide us with new inspiration for service.

Occasionally, people are called to make radical changes. A physician is summoned to step away from a successful medical practice to spearhead the creation of a community clinic in an underserved urban community. Retirement beckons another physician in part to step away from increasingly bureaucratic constraints so she can have more time to donate her skills to people in dire need in overseas missions. Various volunteer opportunities engage people to use their skills in building trades, in emergency response, in tutoring, or in providing Meals on Wheels. The opportunities for service are all around us, sometimes calling in a dramatic way. Yes, people still do such things. Perhaps as you seek discernment God will lay such a radical change on your heart.

For the Discerner

  I. Adventuring with God
  - Review your notes from chapters 2 and 4 on the hero/heroine's journey. Do the insights from the hero/heroine's journey still ring true for you? What adjustments would you make? Be particularly mindful of "helpers" now. What particular forms of assistance do you need to help you in your discernment?
  - Think particularly on the relationship with God that is being revealed in the hero/heroine's journey? Do you identify with any of Campbell's themes to describe your relationship with God at this time— atonement, sacred marriage, or apotheosis? Which one?

  2. Relationship with God
  Utilize the five themes shown on the chart below to describe your relationship with God. What are you discovering about the kind of relationship with God you have presently? What new ways of relating to God are emerging for you?

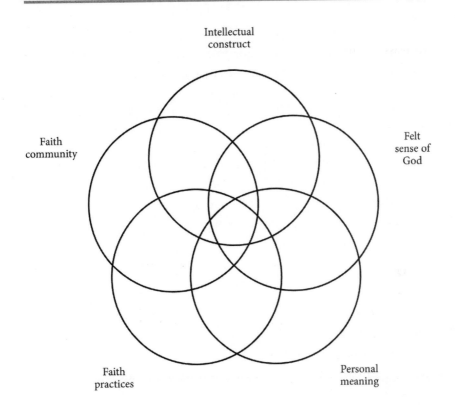

- Felt Sense of God
  How do you experience God? What makes God real to you? Describe your longings with respect to your sense of God's presence?
- Intellectual Construct of God
  What is your understanding of God for your life at the present time? Is it satisfying? What contradictions of living and of understanding about God trouble you? How would you explore your sense of understanding God now?
- Personal Meaning
  Do you usually have a satisfying sense of life meaning? How might your present life decisions be influenced if you put them in the context of asking which outcomes would enhance your sense of meaning and life purpose?
- Faith Practices
  How sustaining are your practices of prayer, worship, and other spiritual disciplines? What is calling to you in terms of faith practice?

- Faith Community

   If you participate in a faith community, are you being stretched toward greater love of God and of humanity? What is your sense of community support for mutual exploration and service? If you do not participate in a faith community now, what would draw you to one?

3. Spiritual Disciplines for Discernment

   Revisit the spiritual and physical disciplines you began in chapter 1 and renewed in chapter 4. Perhaps these patterns are working well for you. Perhaps you would like to adjust what you have planned. Remember "daily" can mean four to five times per week. If you've not been doing some of these, perhaps you tried to commit to too much. There have been many journal exercises since beginning this process. Perhaps that's all that is reasonable to do. Recast the notion of "disciplines" as "time for myself."

4. Just for Fun

   What is one thing you will do in the next week or two, just for fun? This can be very simple, such as going to lunch with a friend, taking a walk, going to a movie.

   Name it _____ Schedule it _____

5. Practicalities

   What information gathering, budget planning, conferring with others, etc., will you do now with reference to your discernment?

   Refer to previous lists. What do you need to accomplish now?

Notes

1. Campbell, M., *Hero with a Thousand Faces*, 245.
2. Ibid.
3. Gawain's adventures are described in Campbell's *Creative Mythology*. See particularly the encounter with the marvel bed, 494–95.
4. Janet K. Ruffing, "Searching for the Beloved: Love Mysticism in Spiritual Direction," in *Spiritual Direction: Beyond the Beginnings*, (New York: Paulist Press, 2000), chap. 4.

8

Listening to
Suffering and Pain

*We . . . are groaning inwardly while we wait for God
to make us God's sons [and daughters] and set our whole body free.
For we have been saved, though only in hope.*
—Rom 8:23–24 (NEB)

"Life is difficult."[1] In 1978, Scott Peck opened his book, *The Road Less Traveled*, with this simple, yet compelling statement that was a revelation to a generation, perhaps too used to things coming their way easily. The beginning stance of Buddhism is that life is suffering.[2] How do we deal with the difficult aspects of life? Perhaps there are very particular issues of human suffering with which we are dealing as we face our discernment questions. How do we listen to our own discomforts and to the suffering of others? How may these deep struggles of soul become a way toward discerning God's movement within our lives?

We know that the major satisfactions in life often require sacrifice. So, we can't base our decisions only on what gives short-term gratification. This may lead to a life less meaningful than a life tested by tough decisions. Yet how do we listen in a spirit of hope to the deep travail that often arises from within our personal lives or in world affairs? Can we trust that through these deep groanings of our spirits, God is actually seeking to communicate with us?

Let us look more deeply into the "sighs too deep for words" (Rom 8:26) or the inward groanings with which we struggle. We cannot avoid such struggles. These pains have messages to reveal to us. Just as physical pain is an indicator that something is wrong in the physical body, emotional suffering can be an indicator that we are being invited to explore personal or communal problems. We can do so by looking for ways that lead to health, to wholeness, or to shalom for all concerned. As we think about relating our discernment tasks to the broadest community concerns, we will be able to anchor our decisions in the hope of participating in life-giving ways to areas of need in our communities and in our world.

The New Testament understanding of salvation is very different than ours. When we now hear the term salvation, don't we think mostly of the afterlife? The afterlife, however, is only one aspect of the term *sozo*, as used in the Bible.

> The root for the word *healing* in New Testament Greek, *sozo*, is the same as that of *salvation* and *wholeness*. Spiritual healing is God's work of offering persons balance, harmony, and wholeness of body, mind, spirit, and relationships through confession, forgiveness, and reconciliation. Through such healing, God works to bring about reconciliation between God and humanity, among individuals and communities, within each person, and between humanity and the rest of creation.[3]

We are invited by Jesus in the New Testament stories and teachings to live lives of health and wholeness. Holiness means wholeness. This kind of wholeness, from the standpoint of promised life eternal, includes the afterlife. But, our quest for *sozo* is also very important in this life, in our concerns in the midst of the struggles of our existence.

The Hebrew concept for this kind of attention to the well-being of the whole of creation is shalom, dwelling in peace and righteousness. Shalom means being in right relationship with all of our fellow creatures. In Christian worship, this breadth of concern is lifted up for us in the prayers of the people.

> Together, let us pray for
> > the people of this congregation . . .
> > those who suffer and those in trouble . . .
> > the concerns of this local community . . .

the world, its people, and its leaders . . .
the church universal—its leaders, its members, and its mission . . .
the communion of saints . . .[4]

We are deeply affected by the ever-widening circles of communal concerns, whether or not we consciously acknowledge these connections. We
are asked in such bidding prayers to pray for each level of concern, from
our family and those closest to us, through each circle of community, until
we reach out to the whole world and even those who have died. As we near
the conclusion of our discernment process, I will invite each of us to place
our decisions within this context. We might diagram this concept of community in the following way:

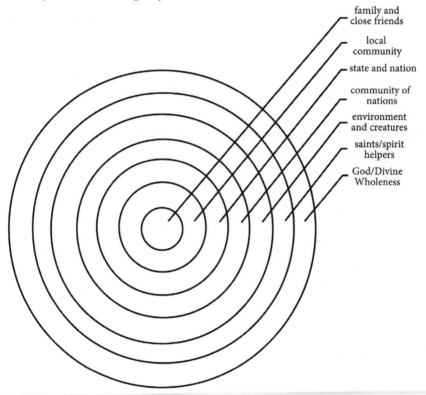

Our discernment will be most meaningful if we have attended to each of
these circles of community. For some people, this will mean engaging very
directly in mission work in the local community or other places of need in
the world. For others it may mean a new commitment to environmental

concerns and care of the creatures of the earth who are our neighbors. In
this chapter I encourage each of us to trust that the concerns pressing on
our hearts are indeed guiding us toward meaningful pathways of prayer
and service.

We will be guided in this exploration by images from Hebrew Scripture, particularly from the Psalms and Prophets. These powerful Scriptures
take us into the heart of community life and struggle. They remind us that
without a healthy social environment, our personal quests for spiritual
peace will be elusive. Long before the contemporary movements of social
awareness, ecopsychology, or environmental concerns, the Psalms and the
Prophets proclaimed the message that all humanity is of one fabric; when
one suffers all suffer. Because nations are capable of gross injustice toward
their own citizens and toward one another, there is an equilibrium of divine
justice built into the essence of human social concerns. Suffering and injustice are signals of disruption in the communal fabric. Our suffering is to
be given voice. Our longings for justice are to rise up to God as incense.
These struggles are God's struggles. Our life as members of the human
community is declared to be the essential background against which all
healthy individual interaction with God and with other human beings takes
place. Quite simply put, we are of necessity bound together in the fabric of
all creation. We can deny those connections or we can affirm that fundamental unity and seek to enhance the inner health and wholeness of the created order.

The Psalms and the Prophets take us into the arena of history, looking for the movement of God beyond our own time, searching for the face
of God within the wars and struggles for freedom and justice in every era
of human endeavors and in every society. The Psalms and the Prophets,
however, are also very personal. They invite us to look into our own hearts
of suffering, longing, and joy. Our hearts long for the right balance between
love and fairness. Although we may find ourselves suffering greatly within
our own lives and within the society in which we live, the Psalms declare
God to be faithful in bringing blessings to us in the very midst of our tri-
als and sufferings, and in restoring joy and peace where there is hatred and
turmoil. God is declared to be faithful to humankind, even when it seems
God is absent.

In addition to looking for meaning within our personal sufferings, our task in this chapter is to find ways to match the inner groanings of our spirits with the sufferings of society and of the earth. As we work with our discernment issues, we cannot find the full peace of God in our decisions until we answer the question, how do our major life decisions contribute to the health of the world? For some people, asking this question will shift the discernment process greatly, causing them to reach out to take a job or volunteer task in the arena of social good. For others, asking the question will not change the direction of the decision so much as enable them to envision their current task as part of the greater whole in which we live. We will look for ways to place our current life transition in the context of our world's needs. Or to put the issue simply, we will try to match our sense of personal meaning in our current life decisions within the larger struggles of our times. We can image our hope with the following diagram:

Our discernment will bear great meaning if we claim God's hope for our world as a community of true peace, right relationship, and shalom. Within God's longing, we will look for a way to relate our own longings of spirit with the world's suffering.

In each stage of my career, it has always been important to me to make a fundamental connection between the obvious tasks of my work and the greater good of the world. In my decade of pastoral ministry in the 1970s, the congregation I served was very supportive of my involvement in many community organizations. I found great fulfillment in creating a community coordinating council to better achieve the community's social service outreach. In my mid-forties when family life was so demanding, I found little time for community service or volunteer work beyond the demands of my academic administrative position. I made peace with the issue of broader service to the world, however, by helping to grow a graduate program in student enrollment. As our department created new work for additional faculty members, we contributed to the economic well-being of the community. I was also able to support the expansion of this program to Japan and Russia. Later in directing a spiritual life center and in developing a seminary program in spiritual formation my own direct work for the world was limited. My indirect work for the good of the world, however, was greatly expanded by mentoring others who were developing their own vocations in spiritual formation outreach. These satisfactions are well known to people in business as they generate greater opportunities for people to be employed. As I face the next vocational transition through formal retirement, I am asking this question again: How can my personal sense of calling contribute to the greater well-being of the world? I don't yet have a clear answer, but I trust that it will come. As we engage our discernment process, this chapter will enable us to think on these issues from the wisdom of the Psalms and the Prophets.

Declaring the Greatness of God

The Psalms declare that our human existence is dependent upon God. The greatness of God is declared again and again throughout the Psalms. God is God and our place is one of radical dependence on God. God's greatness as creator is celebrated in song and dance. The joy of being a creature within such creation is declared. But the majesty and transcendence of God is also declared. God is God, and we are creatures. This perspective is fundamental. Not only can we speak of the communal fabric of human societies, but we must speak of the totality of the universe as one fabric of community. Thus, the fundamental perspective within which we begin to understand our own place is one of acknowledgment of God as Creator, author, progenitor, and essential energy of all that is:

> O sing to the LORD a new song;
>> sing to the LORD, all the earth.
> Sing to the LORD, bless his name;
>> tell of his salvation from day to day.
> Declare his glory among the nations,
>> his marvelous works among all the peoples.
> For great is the LORD, and greatly to be praised;
>> he is to be revered above all gods.
> For all the gods of the peoples are idols,
>> but the LORD made the heavens.
> Honor and majesty are before him;
>> strength and beauty are in his sanctuary.
>
> Ascribe to the LORD, O families of the peoples,
>> ascribe to the LORD glory and strength.
> Ascribe to the LORD the glory due his name;
>> bring an offering, and come into his courts.
> Worship the LORD in holy splendor;
>> tremble before him, all the earth.
>
> Say among the nations, "The LORD is king!
>> The world is firmly established; it shall never be moved.
>> He will judge the peoples with equity."
> Let the heavens be glad, and let the earth rejoice;
>> let the sea roar, and all that fills it;
>> let the field exult, and everything in it.
> Then shall all the trees of the forest sing for joy
>> before the LORD; for he is coming,
>> for he is coming to judge the earth.
> He will judge the world with righteousness,
>> and the peoples with his truth.

—Ps 96

This magnificent hymn sets the context for communal life and personal praise. God is God of creation and of all nations. God judges the nations, God is praised among the trees. For us to celebrate the greatness of God is for us to stand in the proper relationship of the created ones toward the essential force/essence from which creation derives. We find ourselves in the presence of God as essential creator! As in the diagram of the expanding circles of community, engaging God helps us to engage the whole of creation and each level of community. We have the right context to enable us to make good judgments about our prayer and service in each domain, extending from our personal and family concerns to the family of nations. Without acknowledging our absolute dependence on God, we think either too highly or too lowly of ourselves, both as individuals and as societies. With the internal balance that comes from recognizing our essential selfhood in relationship to God, we have the courage to endure suffering, to struggle for justice, and to become agents for God in the world.

Do we understand ourselves as creatures of the Creator, who are possessed with the capacity for communication with the Creator? To do so grants us great dignity as human beings and proper humility before the awesome wonder of the Creator.

Declaring the Sovereignty of God over the Nations

From this personal perspective, Psalm 96 takes us into the arena of nations. It is not only individuals who are declared to be significant in their own sphere of authority, yet must stand in need of surrender to the greatness of God. Nations must also stand in this relationship. God "will judge the peoples with equity." To affirm the great claims in the Psalms as well as the Prophets of a God active in the lives of nations, we must look to the sweep of history, not to the momentary triumphs of destructive and evil forces. This historical perspective, however, is rooted in the proper understanding of the place of human beings within God's creation.

The people of ancient Israel came to see this struggle to be as much one for them as a whole people as for each of them individually before God. The Psalms and the Prophets declare God as ultimate ruler of human affairs. In the Psalms victory for Israel in times of conflict and battle with neighboring nations is celebrated as God's victory:

O sing to the LORD a new song,
    for he has done marvelous things.
His right hand and his holy arm
    have gotten him victory.
The LORD has made known his victory;
    he has revealed his vindication in the sight of the nations.
—Ps 98

When Israel is not victorious, she laments her emptiness. When God seems absent, Israel sings aloud to God to be present within distress:

O God, you have rejected us,
    broken our defenses;
    you have been angry; now restore us!
You have caused the land to quake;
    you have torn it open;
    repair the cracks in it, for it is tottering.
You have made your people suffer hard things;
    you have given us wine to drink that made us reel.
You have set up a banner for those who fear you,
    to rally to it out of bowshot.
Give victory with your right hand, and answer us,
so that those whom you love may be rescued.
—Ps 60:1–5

At first glance, it seems that Israel believes that God favors them against their enemies. Upon closer reading, however, we see the Psalms are full also of lament in times of national and personal defeat. We find Israelites pleading for understanding and insight into the ways of the mighty God. Instead of the simplistic notion that God will always deliver Israel from her enemies, we find a much more complex struggle to understand a sovereign God who though watchful, yet allows nations to govern themselves. We find, in short, the struggle to understand the complexity of human affairs. Such a struggle is very similar to our contemporary difficulties surrounding the dynamics of local, national, and international politics.

Israel's answer involved a historical view based on God's sovereignty. There is a balancing force within all human affairs, whether personal or social. We call this force, "God's justice." God's justice will not let the weak and downtrodden forever stay in that place of suffering. God's justice will not let the rulers maintain their rule forever. Instead, there is a flow of God's mercy and support to those who suffer that will ultimately bring about change and a rebalancing of power. Will this happen now? Perhaps not. Will it happen even within one's life time? Perhaps not. But it will happen as generations play out these dynamics over several centuries. The people of ancient Israel had a sense of history, based upon deliverance to freedom from slavery in Egypt. In the times of renewed distress, the Psalms remember this deliverance, understanding it to be from God. That remembrance gives endurance for present troubles and hope for future renewal of life:

> I cry aloud to God,
>> aloud to God, that he may hear me.
> In the day of my trouble I seek the Lord;
>> in the night my hand is stretched out without wearying;
>> my soul refuses to be comforted.
> I think of God, and I moan;
>> I meditate, and my spirit faints. . . .
>
> I will call to mind the deeds of the LORD;
>> I will remember your wonders of old.
> I will meditate on all your works,
>> and muse on your mighty deeds.
> Your way, O God, is holy.
>> What god is so great as our God?
> You are the God who works wonders;
>> you have displayed your might among the peoples.
> With your strong arm you redeemed your people,
>> the descendants of Jacob and Joseph. . . .
>
> When the waters saw you, O God,
>> when the waters saw you, they were afraid;
>> the very deep trembled. . . .
>
> Your way was through the sea,
>> your path, through the mighty waters;
>> yet your footprints were unseen.
> You led your people like a flock
>> by the hand of Moses and Aaron.
> —Ps 77:1–3, 11–15, 19–20

We cannot fathom this seeming paradox of praise for God in times of victory and in times of defeat without understanding that Israel's history itself oscillated between these two experiences. They were first of all a people that fell into slavery in Egypt. Then, they were brought out of slavery during the period of the conquest of the Canaanites. Ultimately, they became a sovereign nation, with an established monarchy. Then, they were defeated in war, taken into exile into Babylon.

In *Joy Unspeakable*, Barbara Holmes speaks of the indomitable nature of the human spirit evidenced through the moaning cries of the Africans being transported across the ocean in the holds of the slave ships.[5] The words of this Psalm could have been theirs:

> When the waters saw you, O God,
>> when the waters saw you, they were afraid;
>> the very deep trembled. . . .
> Your way was through the sea,
>> your path, through the mighty waters;
>> yet your footprints were unseen.
> —Ps 77:16, 19–20

This profound cry arising from shared suffering sustained the slaves through the time of their complete loss of hope, identity, and culture. We hear that cry through the times of loss for the people of Israel. That cry is universal for the human spirit in times of deep crisis.

In the present times of global crises and threats, the United States of America, as well as other nations, can take solace from the lament of the Psalms. We can also take hope in the principle of God's justice. The Psalms point to the need for nations to approach one another with humility, as the mighty will be brought low and the lowly will be raised up. The Psalms and the Prophets also point to the hope of a renewal, even on the global level, of a climate of peace, justice, and hope. We are emboldened by these images to believe that every small effort of good-will from each of us does contribute to a universal climate of hope and goodwill in our communities, nations, and world. These great Scriptures remind us that life is bitter as well as joyful in the experience of all nations. God is declared faithful in the times of suffering as well as in the times of joy.

The Prophets' message is always one of holding Israel in balance so that in times of prosperity, that prosperity may be shared. In times of loss, God's goodness is remembered. From Isaiah, we read words that are echoed in many other places in the Prophets.

> Shame on you! you who make unjust laws
>   and publish burdensome decrees,
> depriving the poor of justice,
> robbing the weakest of my people of their rights,
> despoiling the widow and plundering the orphan.
> What will you do when called to account,
> when ruin from afar confronts you?
> —Isa 10:1–3 (NEB)

This message is delivered also in Amos:

> You that turn justice upside down and bring righteousness to the ground,
> you that hate a man who brings the wrongdoer to court
> and loathe him who speaks the whole truth:
> for all this, because you levy taxes on the poor
> and extort a tribute of grain from them,
> though you have built houses of hewn stone,
> you shall not live in them,
> though you have planted pleasant vineyards,
> you shall not drink wine from them. . . .
>
> Seek good and not evil,
> that you may live,
> that the LORD the God of Hosts may be firmly on your side,
> as you say he is.
> Hate evil and love good;
> enthrone justice in the courts;
> it may be that the LORD the God of Hosts
> will be gracious to the survivors of Joseph. . . .
>
> I hate, I spurn your pilgrim-feasts;
> I will not delight in your sacred ceremonies.
> When you present your sacrifices and offerings
> I will not accept them,
> nor look on the buffaloes of your shared-offerings.
> Spare me the sound of your songs;
> I cannot endure the music of your lutes.

Let justice roll on like a river
and righteousness like an ever-flowing stream.
—AMOS 5:7–11, 14–15, 21–24 (NEB)

The refrain from these Prophets is not a judgment against wealth, per se, but it is a plea for compassion for those who are weak and suffering within a society. Divine justice as understood in the Psalms and the Prophets makes very practical sense. How can a whole society prosper if the weakest and poorest are not educated? How can justice prevail when particular portions of a society suffer the highest rates of crime?

Do the Prophets give us direct answers to our very real contemporary crises? No, but they do advise us in the strongest way to approach our laws and our society with an attitude of special concern for the weak, the disenfranchised, and the poor. That is the great message that would be given from the Prophets to our current national debates. We do violence to the principles of divine justice, when we approach these debates with attitudes of inflammatory divisiveness and prejudice toward particular groups. The struggle for the Hebrew people, as for us, was to recognize that everyone even within their own nation was actually neighbor, deserving of respect and kindness.

As we move toward completion of our discernment tasks, these principles of fairness and shalom challenge us to ask whether we are seeking balance for our needs and the needs of the whole society. We are called upon to think of the suffering of the whole world, and to inquire how our decisions may relieve some small portion of that suffering rather than contribute to it. We are asked to listen deeply to our own groanings of spirit to discern if those things that deeply disturb our hearts about the wars, economic concerns, and struggles of our neighbors, could be the voice of God calling to us to respond. It is easy to be overwhelmed with these needs. God does not ask that of us. Instead, we are asked to think clearly about how our decisions affect the whole of reality. We may find our answer to be a call to prayer. We may find it to be a call to engagement in new forms of charitable giving. We may find new places for our volunteer efforts. We may make decisions based on environmental concerns and energy efficiencies. While the problems are endless, so are the solutions. To prayerfully consider such engagement is what is asked of each of us.

Discovering God's Comfort in Human Suffering

The same principles that we have been discovering in the Psalms for nations and societies are also applied to the individual. We find that we discover most profoundly who we are, when we understand our relationship to the Creator. From that perspective, we are enabled to embrace God in times of suffering and in times of joy. The Psalms declare that our emotional responses to the struggles of life and to the injustices we experience are valid ways of hearing God's voice. Perhaps this emotional honesty is the reason that the Psalms have been so enduring as the "songbook" not only for the Hebrew people, but also for Christians through the ages.

Spiritual life has been historically understood to involve times of purification or profound suffering, as well as times of joyful illumination and praise in the presence of God. These two perspectives are mirror images in individual life of the times of defeat and victory for the people of Israel. Whether experienced personally or collectively, they are declared in the essential understanding of the Psalms and the Prophets to be two faces of the same God. That image is extremely important to us. Without understanding that God is present in both, we can spend all our lives looking only for the high times of joy and missing God revealed in the very midst of our struggles, sufferings, and turmoil.

The Psalms call us, individually, as well as collectively, to the remembrance of God as Creator. In the greatness of God's creation we find our own life again defined in a positive way:

> Bless the LORD, O my soul.
>   O LORD my God, you are very great.
> You are clothed with honor and majesty,
>   wrapped in light as with a garment.
> You stretch out the heavens like a tent,
>   you set the beams of your chambers on the waters,
> you make the clouds your chariot,
>   you ride on the wings of the wind,
> you make the winds your messengers,
>   fire and flame your ministers. . . .
>
> You cause the grass to grow for the cattle,
>   and plants for people to use,

to bring forth food from the earth,
>   and wine to gladden the human heart,
oil to make the face shine,
>   and bread to strengthen the human heart. . . .

O LORD, how manifold are your works!
>   In wisdom you have made them all;
>   the earth is full of your creatures. . . .

These all look to you
>   to give them their food in due season;
when you give to them, they gather it up;
>   when you open your hand, they are filled with good things.
When you hide your face, they are dismayed;
>   when you take away their breath, they die
>   and return to their dust.
When you send forth your spirit, they are created;
>   and you renew the face of the ground.

May the glory of the LORD endure forever;
>   may the LORD rejoice in his works—
who looks on the earth and it trembles,
>   who touches the mountains and they smoke.
I will sing to the LORD as long as I live;
>   I will sing praise to my God while I have being.
May my meditation be pleasing to him,
>   for I rejoice in the LORD. . . .
Bless the LORD, O my soul.
Praise the Lord!
—Ps 104:1–4, 14–15, 24, 27–35

The Psalms guide us into the celebration of the magnificence of creation. From that perspective, the only attitude we can have is praise and submission to the God of creation. There is really no other response. We witness also our radical dependence upon God for our existence. By the very act of creation, God displays active benevolence to all creatures. Praise is our natural response. Psalm 104 also declares God to be the God of renewal as well as the God of creation. Not only is this world created, but it is being renewed as well. Thus, as creatures of the creation, you and I are also candidates for re-creation and renewal.

From this perspective of profound wonder, awe, and praise, the Psalms are able to be utterly honest about the suffering we experience. They do not shy away from our pain. They face our struggles head-on and cry out our human anguish:

> Save me, O God,
> > for the waters have come up to my neck.
> I sink in deep mire,
> > where there is no foothold;
> I have come into deep waters,
> > and the flood sweeps over me.
> I am weary with my crying;
> > my throat is parched.
> My eyes grow dim with waiting for my God.
> —Ps 69:1–3

> Have mercy on me, O God,
> > according to your steadfast love;
> according to your abundant mercy
> > blot out my transgressions.
> Wash me thoroughly from my iniquity,
> > and cleanse me from my sin.
> —Ps 51:1–2

> As a deer longs for flowing streams,
> > so my soul longs for you, O God.
> My soul thirsts for God,
> > for the living God.
> When shall I come and behold the face of God?
> My tears have been my food day and night,
> while people say to me continually,
> > "Where is your God?"
> —Ps 42:1–3

As the Psalms pour out their lament, they also reach out to God for comfort:

> These things I remember,
> > as I pour out my soul:
> how I went with the throng,
> > and led them in procession to the house of God,
> with glad shouts and songs of thanksgiving,
> > a multitude keeping festival.

Why are you cast down, O my soul,
    and why are you disquieted within me?
Hope in God; for I shall again praise him,
    my help and my God.
—Ps 42:4–6

Throughout the Psalms, we find the affirmation of clinging to God in times of celebration and in times of distress. There is a raw honesty in the Psalms that can be disquieting to contemporary readers. The Psalms lay bare the human struggle to understand the ways of God when all goes wrong. They lament the fragility of human relationships. Praying with the Psalms enables us to pray through our own suffering and pain and the pain we experience on behalf of a suffering world.

Diane is in her mid fifties. She finds one of her most significant ways of understanding this dual nature of reality in her work with people who are grieving the loss of a loved one. For twenty years, she has worked in some way with grief counseling organizations, sometimes as a paid employee, sometimes as a volunteer. She has sought out such organizations when living on the West Coast and in the Midwest, in urban and small town settings. She helped develop a program for children who have lost a sibling and for their parents. Why has this work been so important for her? Because she says, it helps her be in touch with the fragility of life. Diane has discovered that intersection where the suffering of others in the world links with her own inward groaning of spirit. In our current tasks of discernment, let us look for our direction from both our struggles in the depths as well as our rejoicing in the heights of our human existence.

God's Ultimate Victory

The Psalms and the Prophets take not only a historical perspective on God's past relationship with Israel, but they also take a prophetic perspective on God's ultimate victory within human affairs. Some of the most significant words of hope ever written are found in Isaiah. Those words took root very deeply in me as a child, in their promise spoken every Christmas Eve. They motivate me still with hope for a new future, promised in the fullness of time, to bring all of humanity into a relationship of peace, justice, and joy in the midst of earthly life.

The wolf shall live with the lamb,
    the leopard shall lie down with the kid,
the calf and the lion and the fatling together,
    and a little child shall lead them.
The cow and the bear shall graze,
    their young shall lie down together;
    and the lion shall eat straw like the ox.
The nursing child shall play over the hole of the asp,
    and the weaned child shall put its hand on the adder's den.
They will not hurt or destroy
    on all my holy mountain;
for the earth will be full of the knowledge of the LORD
    as the waters cover the sea.
—ISA 11:6–9

For the Discerner

Take a moment just to listen to your heart when you read those words from Isaiah. Through the inspiration and confrontation of such prophetic utterances, we are still inspired to look toward the future manifestation of human and earthly life with possibilities for greater love, justice, and peace within human societies and nations.

And God asks no less from us now.

I. Use Scripture to Find Discernment Themes
Pick two or three of the Scriptures cited in this chapter. Dwell with them for a week. Let them help you attend to the following themes:
- What personal pains and sufferings are on your heart? Ask yourself what these inward groanings may be seeking to tell you about your discernment themes.
- What pains and sufferings on behalf of the world are particularly on your heart at this time? Ask yourself what these groanings on behalf of the suffering of the world may be seeking to tell you about your discernment themes.

2. Four Ways to Explore Personal and Social Themes
Matthew Fox developed a profound way of exploring our spiritual

issues in his book, *Original Blessing.*[6] He spoke of four major themes that help focus our spiritual lives—the *Via Positiva*; *Via Negativa*; *Via Creativa*; and *Via Transformativa*. These themes open up the personal and social concerns we have explored through the Psalms and the Prophets. I invite you to think on these themes.

- *Via Positiva*

  How do you celebrate your life as a human being, created by God? In the creation story, when human beings are created, they are said by God to be "very good." All the created order is given this same affirmation. What aspects of life as a creature of God's creation inspire you, fill you with joy and hope, uplift your spirit? Do you spend time in these activities regularly? Do you need to make more time to experience these joys? How will you do so?

- *Via Negativa*

  What aspects of human existence create pain and suffering for you? These can be very particular, such as health problems or emotional struggles or addictions. They can also be related to the suffering of others within the world. This may be an intense sense of suffering for the ecological, political, or economic health of our world. Name your particular sufferings. What helps you to deal with this sense of suffering on a daily basis? Do you pray in a certain way, talk with colleagues, take these concerns to worship? Do you have other means of gaining insight about these? How does this awareness affect your present discernment?

- *Via Creativa*

  Fox's thesis is that by attending deeply to the *Via Positiva* and the *Via Negativa* our creative energy is unleashed. As you reflect upon both your list of issues in the *Via Positiva* and in the *Via Negativa*, allow creative responses to emerge from your own spirit. Listen to how you respond to suffering in ways that draw from your sense of blessing as a creature of the universe. Is God calling you toward a creative service that seems different than the ones you've been considering in your discernment process? Let yourself be open to these surprises. Then, ask how these insights affect the discernment themes with which you've been working.

- *Via Transformativa*

  The *Via Transformativa* is very similar to Campbell's theme of sharing the elixir with the world. Fox contends that we are made by God to be discontent until we can see our own small efforts in the *Via Creativa* relating clearly to the life of the world. How does our life of work and service relate to the transformation—the health, the salvation—of the world? Entertaining this question may change nothing about the actual work in which we are engaging, but it will give us a sense of contribution to the larger stream of life of which we are a part.

3. Name Specific Ways to Serve

   Use the following diagram and name specific ways of service, prayer, or charitable giving to which you are being called in each circle for the next year. Be as specific as possible:

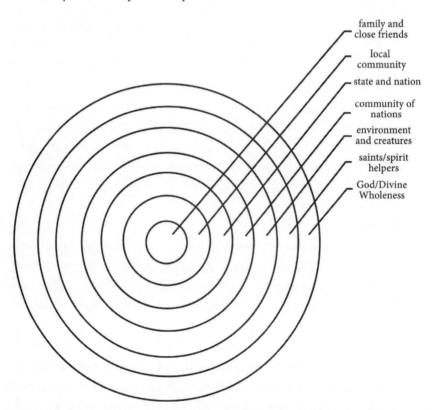

Which arenas are most prominent for you as you consider your major discernment issues? Are there areas of community service that become clearer? What information do you need to gather regarding working, volunteering, or charitable giving, as you explore these issues?

4. Just for Fun

What is one thing you will do just for fun? This can be very simple, such as going to lunch with a friend, taking a walk, going to a movie.

Name it _____ Schedule it _____

5. Practicalities

What information gathering, budget planning, conferring with others, etc., do you need to accomplish with reference to your discernment?

Revisit your list from previous chapters. What needs to be done now? What goes into your information file?

Notes

I. M. Scott Peck, M.D., *The Road Less Traveled, 25th Anniversary Edition: A New Psychology of Love, Traditional Values and Spiritual Growth* (New York, Touchstone, 2003), 15.

2. The first of the four noble truths of Buddhism: see Huston Smith, *The World's Religions* (San Francisco: HarperSanFrancisco, 1991), 99.

3. "Healing Services and Prayers, Introduction," *The United Methodist Book of Worship* (Nashville: The United Methodist Publishing House, 1992), 613–14.

4. *The United Methodist Hymnal, Book of United Methodist Worship* (Nashville, The United Methodist Publishing House, 1989), 877.

5. Barbara Holmes, *Joy Unspeakable: Contemplative Practices of the Black Church* (Minneapolis: Fortress Press, 2004).

6. Matthew Fox, *Original Blessing: A Primer in Creation Spirituality Presented in Four Paths, Twenty-Six Themes, and Two Questions* (New York: Tarcher/Putnam, 2000).

9

Seeking Forgiveness
and Inner Healing

You are the salt of the earth; but if salt has lost its taste,
how can its saltiness be restored? It is no longer good for anything,
but is thrown out and trampled under foot.
*—*Matt 5:13

Seeking Personal Wholeness

"You are the salt of the earth," Jesus proclaims to those who seek him. This statement in the Gospel of Matthew follows the Beatitudes, the profound litany of high calling to which Jesus summons us. Salt gives flavor. And, in Jesus' time, it was a primary preservative of food. Jesus invites us to be full of life, robust in flavor. As we make a major life transition, there are frequently issues from our past relationships or work experiences that seem unresolved. These inhibit us from being "salt," from offering our unique flavor to life. The spice we might give to enrich the lives of those around us is inhibited by the way past hurts or failures may weigh upon us. These issues may press on us in ways that hold us back from the new life that is calling us. Are there areas of inner struggle, or even guilt for past errors, that may be keeping us from the good flavor of life? This description of people as the salt to the world is followed in the same Scripture passage with the grand hope that we be "light" to the world. "Let your light shine before others, so that they may see your good works and give glory to your Father in heaven." Let us complete our discernment reflections so that we offer greater light and salt to the world.

Over the years, we have all made errors of judgment. We have left undone that which we ought to have done and done that which we ought not to have done. Years later we may experience remorse for some of these actions and the memory of such wrongs may weigh heavily upon us. It took Jacob twenty-one years to decide to return to his homeland and seek to reconcile with his brother, Esau. Perhaps there are struggles from the near or distant past that weigh upon our hearts.

We may also be haunted by wrongs done to us. Are we carrying scars of pain and hurt with us? How heavy is that "baggage" from the past? The memory of old resentments and hurts can easily limit our expression of "light," health, *sozo* for our service in the world. Jacob carries such a sense of guilt for his action toward Esau for twenty-one years. We can see his efforts at offering recompense to Esau in his return. Once Jacob actually encounters Esau, he discovers Esau has long ago forgiven him. Esau overcame the lack of formal birthright that Jacob had stolen so many years before. Jacob's return is highly ironic, perhaps even humorous. He sends all of his herds, his wealth, and his huge extended family in front of him. It is as if he is making an offering to Esau of any of Jacob's wealth if he wishes to claim it for himself. We can imagine Esau wondering what strange gifts these are, until finally Jacob reveals himself. Then, rather than the confrontation Jacob expects, he is lovingly embraced by Esau as his long-lost brother (Gen 33:1–11).

This story of profound forgiveness and reconciliation foreshadows Jesus' story of the prodigal son (Luke15:11–32). Before the son reaches home, his father has already rushed out to greet him and reconcile with him.

Whether we think of Jacob or of the son, it is clear that each has carried a great burden of regret. Each is given new life by receiving in person the blessing that had been given inwardly long ago by Esau and by the father. As we move toward completion of the present discernment process, it is very helpful to examine the past. Do we find ourselves in the position of Esau for some wrongs inflicted upon us? Have we been able

to forgive or do we still carry resentments? Are there issues of unre-
dresssed injustice that haunt us? Perhaps we are carrying guilt for some
past deeds toward others.

There may also be areas of regret that we carry with us. In our reflections through these discernment exercises, it is clear that we have said no to
certain possibilities in order to say yes to others. There may be some regret
for roads not taken. We may doubt the wisdom of our past decisions and
self-doubt may have crept into our sense of personal identity. Do we need
to make peace with some of those earlier choices before being free to
embrace current options?

Remember those words of Jesus that we previously discussed:

"You must be born of spirit and water."

"You must be born over again."

We are truly invited in this creative life of the Spirit to let ourselves be
healed, so that we can be new vessels of light and hope as the years roll by
and as new life calling summons us.

We have been exploring both our life of inner spirituality and our life
in community. We have spoken of these domains in several ways. One way
was to use Ernest Boyer's image of the spirituality of the center and the
spirituality of the edge. We have spoken of the solitary call to adventure and
we have described the spirituality of weaving the fabric of community. We
have described loving God with all our heart and mind and soul and
strength and our neighbor as ourselves. The diagram on the following page
helps us think about particular areas of past hurt, choices, or needs for
inner healing. Most of us will be able to identify one or two areas in which
we carry issues from our past. Now is the opportunity to pray through to
resolution so that our "light" can shine more boldly.

Inner Healing, Forgiveness, and Reconciliation

Do we actually believe in the possibility of inner healing and forgiveness?
Is it truly possible to forgive and to be forgiven? Is it possible to be released
from the suffering of memories? Is it possible to be reconciled to our life
choices and to other people? Christian faith speaks of the forgiveness of
sin. Psychological process speaks of the healing of inner wounds. Buddhism speaks of the need to understand and release our attachments and

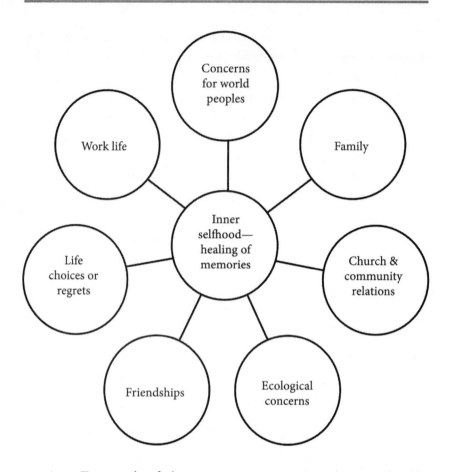

aversions. From each of these perspectives, we are seeking to describe aspects of inner struggle that linger, resisting easy release, and for which there may be remorse or pain. Inner wounds often contain memories; yet, like an unhealed physical wound, these memories continue to evoke emotion, long after they have occurred. Whenever a similar experience crosses our awareness or we open to a similar emotion, the inner wound can become raw again. For now, let us simplify our understanding of these dynamics and call each lingering sense of sin or each major regret or each inner wound a suitcase—a piece of baggage we continue to carry with us.

In order to be freed from the burden of this baggage, we need to open up the suitcase, look clearly at the contents, offer these painful circumstances to God, and receive deep release. Can we allow ourselves to let go? Are there particular amends we need to make in order to find release? Or can deep prayer release us, enable us to let go of this piece of baggage and walk in newness of life? Many of these issues linger with us because they hold very deep trauma. There may be a whole set of memories, particularly if we have been victimized by early childhood abuse, as well as an emotional response pattern that continues to haunt us. Finally, since these issues bring so much hurt with them, we are usually also in an internal battle, and frequently suffer self-criticism for not being able to rid ourselves of such pain. Deep healing allows us to relive the pain momentarily, find new understanding, and release this past hurt into Christ's healing love. We are able to gain insight because the emotions, the memories, and the habits of thought surrounding these wounds are opened up to healing love. The inner wound is revealed as multiple aspects of memory, emotion, and thoughts all held together as a deep hurt. The wound is opened, the contents revealed, repentance offered, necessary amends are made, and reconciliation is revealed. Newness of life can be received!

The following diagram may help us understand the nature of such wounds.

The core is an experience or set of experiences, in which we have suffered pain or inflicted it. Or that central core may be a life choice in the past that

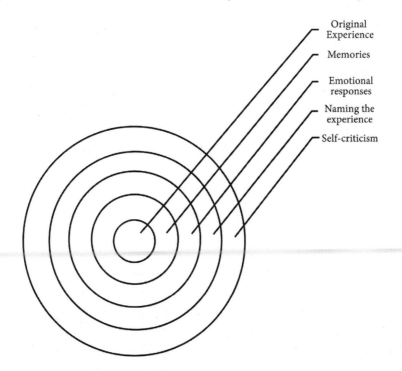

Original Experience

Memories

Emotional responses

Naming the experience

Self-criticism

we now regret. Furthermore, an inner wound accumulates additional memories that reinforce our original sense of hurt received or inflicted. Emotions
gather around each of these additional memories, as well as the original events.
Usually deep fear arises as well. We are worried or anxious. We doubt our
capacities to make good choices as a result. Guilt or shame may accompany
these emotions. At some point in our struggle with this deep wound, we begin
to give a name to the feelings. Some of this naming can be quite helpful. In
fact, we may be naming something now as we read these descriptions.

By acknowledging our sin or hurt, we have opened the opportunity for
healing and reconciliation. Usually, however, we just keep repeating this
name to ourselves. The inner wounds become major building blocks of our
identity. Usually, we carry many of these wounds in our own sense of selfhood. And each of them brings with it a few comments of negative self-
criticism. When we examine our true sense of selfhood, we are each very
likely to discover a few inner messages, which we repeat to ourselves at least
weekly. Many of them are inwardly repeated a few times a day. "I'm stu-
pid." "I'm fat." "I'm awful." "I'm selfish." "I screwed up." While there may
be some truth to these kinds of statements, there is also a lot of fallout to
our self-image. We are swimming around in a sea of unprocessed negativ-
ity. At the core of such internalized self statements is some hurt received
or inflicted, together with unredeemed pain. It is no accident that sin and
death are so closely associated in Scripture (see Rom 8). Sin becomes death.
It robs us of life. The notion of the inner wounding helps us understand
this insidious aspect of sin in our effort to live faithfully.

As we enter into a new phase of life, we are in a unique position to
release negative inner processes. We are offered new life in all aspects of our
being, even our innermost thoughts. These principles are illustrated very
dramatically in the life of Chris, a woman in her forties, who is moving into
a new calling in her work. Her vision for the new work is changing her self-
understanding, her family relationships, and her social relationships. Chris
has been a significant member of her community, church, and social circle
for many years. Her vision of creating a new community-based ministry is
moving her into a role of leadership that shifts her friendships and family
roles. While working on several fronts to bring this new work into being,
she has been experiencing disturbing dreams. Sometimes they have been
frightening, sometimes comforting and hopeful. It seems clear that her

deep spirit is causing her to pause before her new work can be undertaken. It has been a difficult several months, as she has engaged the inward work of naming old hurts, listening to them, and opening to new perceptions. Sometimes it has felt like a dark night of the soul—in which her pathway would be completely lost. She has worked on her issues in counseling and spiritual direction, and recently she discovered a dream group, as well. In reflecting on one of her dreams, Chris recognized the depth of the life transition she is experiencing: "I know that I will be the same person, but also I realize that if I receive this transformation and surrender my being to God that I will be different. I won't be the same. The carefree part of me—the wild, spontaneous, mysterious 'college girl' part of me is leaving. It is time. It's just strange." The way is clearing. Her dreams now point to new life emerging. She is also sharing her vision for her new life work and finding support in many amazing ways. The inward transformation has been essential preparation for the work to which she is called.

As we make changes from one phase of life to another, as we move through a major life-decision process, it is important to do some inner housecleaning. We may even be called to a time of very deep inner work, as has been the case for Chris. As our sense of self-identity is shifting and changing, perhaps we are more aware of some of the past hurt and pain with which we have been burdened. Perhaps memories of such troubling experiences are coming into our awareness through this time of transition. A faith stance toward life invites us not to push those deep concerns aside, but rather to embrace their pain and to bring them to awareness, forgiveness, and reconciliation.

> From now on, therefore, we regard no one from a human point of view; even though we once knew Christ from a human point of view, we know him no longer in that way. So if anyone is in Christ, there is a new creation: everything old has passed away; see, everything has become new! All this is from God, who reconciled us to himself through Christ, and has given us the ministry of reconciliation; that is, in Christ God was reconciling the world to himself, not counting their trespasses against them, and entrusting the message of reconciliation to us. So we are ambassadors for Christ, since God is making his appeal through us; we entreat you on behalf of Christ, be reconciled to God. For our sake he made him to be sin who knew no sin, so that in him we might become the righteousness of God.
>
> —2 COR 5:16–21

You see it is not only for ourselves that we are asked to be reconciled. We are asked by God to receive reconciliation with God so that we can be fully, freely ourselves in Christ and ambassadors for God in the world. So, as we reach out to God to claim the new life being promised, we are asked to present ourselves for inner healing, forgiveness, and reconciliation. What an amazing thing. God wants us to be redeemed at each crossroads of our life journeys, just as has been the case for Chris.

For the Discerner

1. Baggage from the Past

   What baggage do you bring into the current journey? Are there circumstances you need to confess and release from the past? Are there actual people you need to contact? Are you ready for a ritual for release and healing? Are there hurts you have inflicted that you are ready to release? Are there hurts from others to you that continue to hold you back?

2. Roads Not Taken

   Are there roads not taken because of your life choices that you now regret? Are there one or more decisions you would like to do in a different way? Can you actually now embrace a modified version of such a choice? Or must you find a way to release your regret over such choice? Are you willing to bring that choice to Christ for release and reconciliation?

3. Identifying Past Regrets and Hurts

   How does the diagram on the next page help you identify any other areas in which there are particular past regrets or hurts that you continue to carry with you?

4. Healing Inner wounds

   Pick a way to seek inner healing and reconciliation. Use one or more of the following exercises to help you pray through these areas of inner wounds.
   - Seek Counseling

     If you identify deep inner wounding or trauma, you may need to enter into counseling or take these problems to your spiritual director. Perhaps you have not faced these difficulties before. Perhaps you

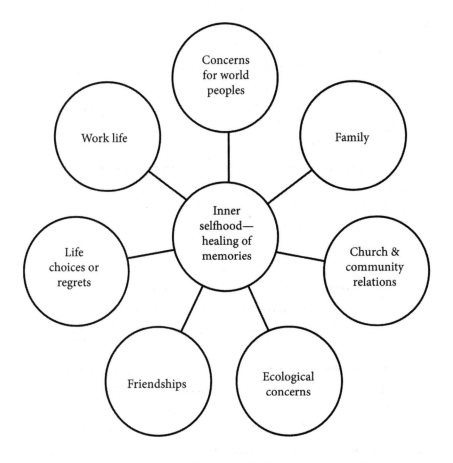

are having a hard time addressing the hurts and pains that are coming to your awareness. It is often critical to work directly with such a deep issue before moving onward with a major life-decision process. Perhaps this is the time you will lay aside any other concerns and enter into a sustained counseling relationship for inner healing. That, by itself, would be a very good outcome to this discernment journey.

- Enter into Prayer

  Find a time to enter into a period of sustained prayer this week. Bring your baggage to Jesus, Sophia/Wisdom, Mary, or another wisdom figure. Center yourself in the unconditional love offered by the holy one. Unpack your baggage, bringing forth memories, hurts, sighs too deep for words, and allow new insights to arise. Receive the new life promised. Write down what you discover.

- Visit Jesus

  Visit with Jesus at the well. Read John 4:1–26. The Samaritan woman was approached by Jesus for a drink of water. In your imagination, sit with Jesus at the well and pour out your heart. Listen for his understanding, your release from the past, and suggestions regarding your future.

- Pray with Your Group

  If you are working with a small group, perhaps you would like your group to participate in a ritual of forgiveness and reconciliation, offering the laying on of hands and prayer for one another. You do not need to reveal your hurt, although you may wish to do so. The Holy Spirit promises to be with us when we offer such gentle prayer to one another.

- Seek Formal Reconciliation

  You may be sensing the need for a formal time of confession and reconciliation facilitated by your pastor, spiritual director, or a spiritual friend. Make an appointment, stating your desire for a formal ritual of forgiveness and/or reconciliation. Make careful preparations, perhaps bringing a few small items, photographs, or journal reflections to help you articulate the circumstances that you continue to carry with you. Ask for prayer and perhaps anointing with oil as an act of release and renewal in Christ.

5. Just for Fun

   What is one thing you will do just for fun this week or next? This can be very simple, such as going to lunch with a friend, taking a walk, going to a movie.

   Name it _____ Schedule it _____

6. Practicalities

   What information gathering, budget planning, conferring with others, etc., do you need to accomplish in the next few weeks with reference to your discernment?

   Revisit your lists from previous chapters. What needs to be done now? What goes into your information file?

10

Being Embodied:
The Importance of Place

Location, Location, Location

Whatever we human beings are—however we envision the transcendence of the soul—while we are alive in the flesh, we are subject to the joys and limitations of time and space. Spirit may soar through time and space in our imagination, but we must daily eat, sleep, and be located in a very particular time and place. A sure sign of the limitations of embodiment is how frequently we allow ourselves to be tyrannized by time.

Psalm 84 celebrates the realities of our relationship to our bodies and to place. Psalm 84 also celebrates God's location within our earthly domain:

How lovely is your dwelling place,
O LORD of hosts!
My soul longs, indeed it faints
for the courts of the LORD;

My heart and my flesh sing for joy
　　to the living God.

Even the sparrow finds a home,
　　and the swallow a nest for herself,
　　where she may lay her young,
at your altars, O LORD of hosts,
　　my King and my God.
Happy are those who live in your house,
　　ever singing your praise.
—Ps 84:1–4

God's own transcendence is envisioned as finding a place within the temple in a specific location on the earth. Within the temple is a place for God, for sparrows, and for human beings.

Many of the significant stories of Scripture involve particular places. Particular destinations are very often mentioned in Scripture stories. Abraham and Sarah are on the way to a particular place chosen for them by God. Jacob flees to the land of his uncle. Joseph is sold into slavery in Egypt. Famine drives people from place to place in the stories of the Bible. Naomi first leaves Nazareth and then returns because of the ravages of famine. When Naomi begins her return, her daughters-in-law must decide whether or not to go with her or to return to their own mothers' houses, each in a particular country. Joseph, the father of Jesus, is warned in dreams to flee into Egypt and then to return to Nazareth. Place is critical.

Listening Places and Living Places

Belden Lane has written a compelling statement on the significance of place in his book *The Solace of Fierce Landscapes: Exploring Desert and Mountain Spirituality.*[1] The book reminds the reader of the many uses of geography in Scripture. For example, Lane cites a reference mentioning that the common "word for mountain (*hār*) appears no less than 520 times in the Hebrew scriptures."[2] Mountains, valleys, and deserts appear throughout biblical narratives. Lane illumines our discussion about the spirituality of the edge and the spirituality of the center. "Desert and mountain places, located on the margins of society, are locations of choice in luring God's people to a deeper understanding of who they are. Yahweh frequently moves to the boundary in order to restore the center, calling a broken people back to justice and compassion."[3]

In this chapter we will consider location in two different ways. One idea of place comes from the following question: Is there a place at the boundaries of our life where we may need to go on retreat in order to complete our discernment process? To use Lane's image, is there a special boundary place for revelation from God that we need to visit in order to listen for God's guidance? The second idea of place is the following: What actual physical places might we need to visit in order to discover if we are being called to live out our next phase of life in that location? When Ruth and I were considering two possibilities in late fall 1993, we knew that we had to visit both regions in order to complete our discernment process. This was the decision that ultimately took us from California to Indiana. It was critical for us to experience the work environment, real estate realities, and schools in the two communities. How would each affect our family life? How might our individual vocational aspirations be served in each situation? So, as we near the completion of this discernment process, let us be mindful of the significance of place. Location is important. Feeling our way into relationships with persons and places relevant to our decision is vital. Honoring our body's reaction to issues of place is a significant part of the decision process. We are embodied. Place is important.

In *The Spell of the Sensuous*, David Abram offers a helpful description of the way our own language has cut us off from paying attention to the physical nature of our existence.[4] He discusses pictographic languages and ancient forms of human language as deeply embedded in the geographic realities of particular places. To this day the Aboriginal people of Australia cannot fully speak their language apart from the land. He describes quite vividly how the language of his Aboriginal companion changed when this individual returned to the Aboriginal homeland. Pictographic forms of writing such as Chinese contain visual cues related directly to physical shapes. With languages of alphabetic form, our concepts can be separated from the realities of people, objects, and place. This abstraction of language has contributed to an alienation from bodily awareness for many people. The mind-body movement is providing methods for renewing the connection between the awareness of our minds and the signals emanating moment to moment from our bodies. So, as we begin to formulate a plan for our next phase of life, let us be in "place," by observing what our sensitivities tell us about such places and communities and bringing those observations into our decision process. Also, we should pay attention to the cues arising from our bodies as we complete our discernment process.

Incarnation

Another way to speak of these deep mysteries is to speak of the summons of Christ to be incarnated in our lives at each of our particular crossroads. It is to an individual, Mary, that the angel Gabriel speaks in making the bold pronouncement that she will be mother to the one to be named Jesus (meaning he will save the people from their sins).[5] God wants to be similarly embodied in our own living for the health of the world. Recall our previous discussions on the meaning of salvation as health. Our life stories find ultimate meaning in participating in God's ongoing story of seeking to provide *sozo*, health, for our communities and our world. God uses our hands, our hearts, our daily work to create the streets, the food, the commerce, the means of transportation and communication through which the world functions. It is through the human spirit that God works for beauty, for joy produced by the arts and entertainment, for inspiration provided by music, and for the safety provided by our police, military, public health workers, and fire departments. Each of us is important to the well-being of our communities through work, community service, and volunteer efforts. We find our ultimate peace by sensing our own cooperation with the hope of God for the health of our communities and the world. As our own skills resonate with the clarity of God's song, our hearts will experience living joy within our own bodies.

We are creatures who live in a single skin throughout our lives. Our own consciousness is embodied in a skin that grows wrinkly over time. Our aging is obvious, no matter how much we might try to resist it. Our nearest cousins in terms of mammalian skin are elephants.[6] Can we be at home in our own skins, our own bodies, adjusting to the changes the various seasons of life bring to us? These skins of ours have been in many places already. We have been sensitized to health-giving and health-robbing environments. An important part of our discernment can be our physical responses as we entertain options, particularly if they involve different geographical locations.

How does God want to be birthed through us in this current decision process? How does God want to be incarnated—to take on human flesh—within our life stories now? How may our decision contribute to the health and wholeness of the world? Where will these tasks take place? Can we each trust our "hearts" to help in this decision, by literally experiencing our sense of physical well-being as we consider different options?

Community, Community, Community

A number of years ago, I took on positions in which I would occasionally be able to hire a new employee. I learned very early in such hiring processes to greatly value the communal nature of such decisions. My decisions were always better if they were made in a team context. If others could be involved in interviews and in the decision process, we noticed different aspects of resumes and of candidates. I became fascinated with the people who came forward for such positions. They were always qualified. But, they were always qualified in different ways. It became a real joy to observe how each applicant for the same clearly articulated job would begin to determine different specifics for the job because of each one's unique qualifications. My understanding of the potentials of a position always changed during the interviews. The process of candidates actually presenting themselves enhanced the potential of these jobs. The honoring of their unique gifts, accrued through their uniquely lived and uniquely embodied life experience, offered *sozo*.

Are we able to be in a climate of such mutual respect as we work toward our present decision? Will the community of persons involved around us enable our hearts and flesh to sing for joy for some years into the future? Is there enough goodwill present that we believe the inevitable clashes of personality and the inevitable misunderstandings of expectations can be navigated in a climate of care? All of these concerns, I believe, resonate in this open-ended notion of listening with our "heart" in such decision processes. May we listen well.

Does our present living situation support the calling of God now appearing in our hearts? In working with people through discernment processes over many years, I've been impressed by the importance of place. Is this a time to stay rooted in a community, perhaps shifting primary vocational or volunteer activities? Or is this a time for a major move? Each decision has significant implications. Neither is easy as in either case new communities of support must be developed. Place is important.

Educating Our Hearts for Listening

Many years ago, I began offering an advent retreat based on the annunciation story. Frequently, I called this retreat: "Meeting the Angel." As we seek to listen to the embodied/physical realities of our decision process, there is no better story of Scripture to help us educate our hearts in how to listen. As we explore the steps for discernment that Mary experiences in this story, it is important to also see the context that she brings to the incarnation. That context is expressed most fully in her song, the Magnificat. In the Magnificat, the full notion of Jesus' contribution to the health of the nations is made clear. The ramifications of what Matthew Fox has called the *ViaTransformativa* are obvious. This birth is not just for Mary's personal joy. It is for the *sozo* of the world. So, as we make our small contribution to the world's *sozo* in this time of decision, the Magnificat is a reminder that we will not be fully satisfied with our choices unless we can link our decisions with the actual well-being of others. When we make that linkage, even if it is primarily within the ponderings of our own heart, then our heart and flesh can sing for joy more fully.

Mary's Song—The Magnificat

And Mary said:

Tell out, my soul, the greatness of the Lord,
rejoice, rejoice, my spirit, in God my savior;
so tenderly has [God] looked upon [this] servant, humble as she is.

For, from this day forth,
all generations will count me blessed,
so wonderfully has [God] dealt with me, the Lord, the Mighty One.

[God's] name is Holy;
[God's] mercy sure from generation to generation
toward those who [hold God in awe];
the deeds [of God's] own right arm . . . disclose [wondrous] might:

the arrogant of heart and mind [have been] put to rout,
[God has brought down monarchs] from their thrones,
but the humble have been lifted high.

The hungry [have been] satisfied with good things,
the rich sent empty away.

[God is placed on] the side of [the servant,] Israel . . . ;
firm in the promise to our forefathers,

[God] has not forgotten to show mercy to Abraham
and his children's children, for ever.

—LUKE 1:46–55 (NEB)

As we weigh our decisions, we need to think about how they participate in assisting God in bringing about a world of peace, justice, and hope for all people. In the context of our life how do we also contribute to the ongoing flow of generation after generation? How do we honor the simple and the hungry? Perhaps our answers are very direct in the precise nature of our living, working, and service. Our lives may be lived in direct service to people in need. Or perhaps our answers are more indirect and yet very important toward this vision of peace raised in Mary's song.

Elder Birth and Virgin Birth

The Annunciation

In the sixth month the angel Gabriel was sent from God
to a town in Galilee called Nazareth,
with a message for a girl betrothed to a man named Joseph,
a descendant of David;
the girl's name was Mary.

The angel went in and said to her,
"Greetings, most favored one! The Lord is with you."

But she was deeply troubled by what he said
and wondered what this greeting might mean.
Then the angel said to her,
"Do not be afraid, Mary, for God has been gracious to you;
you shall conceive and bear a son, and you shall give him the name Jesus.
He will be great; he will bear the title
'Son of the Most High';
the Lord God will give him the throne of his ancestor David,
and he will be king over Israel for ever;
his reign shall never end."

"How can this be?" said Mary;
"[I am still a virgin]."

The angel answered,
"The Holy Spirit will come upon you,
and the power of the Most High will overshadow you;
and for that reason the holy child to be born will be called,
'Son of God.'

Moreover your kinswoman Elizabeth has herself conceived a son in her old age;
and she who is reputed barren is now in her sixth month,
for God's promises can never fail."

"Here am I," said Mary;
"I am the Lord's servant; as you have spoken, so be it."
Then the angel left her.

—LUKE 1:26–38 (NEB)

On Christmas Eve, this Scripture is usually read, beginning just as written here—"In the sixth month . . . ." Whose sixth month is this? What is the Scripture talking about? We've heard it so often, we may have stopped being curious. This sixth month being announced is only made clear if we read earlier or later in the narrative. The "sixth month" is the sixth month of pregnancy of Elizabeth, Mary's cousin. Elizabeth was believed to be barren. In fact, she is "in her old age," or elderly by the standards of her time. We have a marvelous gift in this story and in the strange way the Scripture is divided. Mary's story is not isolated. Her story of birthing new life is seen in the context of the miraculous pregnancy of her kinswoman Elizabeth. The stories of Mary and Elizabeth are yoked together. In fact, as we'll see in looking at the process of Mary's assent to bear this pregnancy, she doesn't say yes until after she hears of Elizabeth's pregnancy.

Christian tradition has so focused on the aspect of virgin birth, or birth from youth, that we have tended to neglect the miracle of birth, so frequently mentioned in Scripture, by elder women—birth from those deemed not able to conceive. By yoking these miracle births together, we can readily see that throughout our life journeys we are invited to continue to participate in the miracles of God. Elder birth is just as amazing, according to Scripture, as virgin birth. No matter our age, we can be used for the new birth of God's goodness into the world. We also see the community aspect of God's miracles announced in the clearest possible way. If this new stage of life is truly from God, it will be confirmed in the vision, hopes, and dreams, not only of one individual, but in the hearts of others. We will be looking for confirmation of our decision processes in the prayerful intent of others, especially those most directly affected by our decisions. Hence, in discerning the move from California to Indiana in 1993 that I've mentioned, weighing the aspect of a community of people with whom to live and serve was critical. Particularly critical was the discernment Ruth and I did together as a couple for our sense of best placement for our family and for the well-being and vocational advancement of each other. We were Mary and Elizabeth to each other in that time of great change. Do you have a Mary or Elizabeth to assist you?

Often in couple relationships, there can be major conflicts about our life decisions. Sometimes, it seems as if there can be no way to bridge two vocational pathways or the implications of broader family concerns. Our task then is to continue to be true to our own sense of calling, but also to be fully committed to our partner. Just when it seems impossible, a third way will often arise that will provide a solution that was eluding us. That surprising solution can only arise if we approach our decision in honesty, in hope, and in humility, with an open spirit for being surprised. Such a surprise may include making way for dual households for a time with one partner commuting great distances. Such surprises may involve staying in one place for the sake of the family or moving and being amazed at a better circumstance for children than was available in the original location. How will we be Mary and Elizabeth to each other, embodying our life transitions, even when the realities of physical location seem insurmountable?

Praying the Story of Mary and Elizabeth for Discernment

I will offer some reflections on the story to assist us in seeing how it helps us to listen well for discernment.

The Annunciation

In the sixth month the angel Gabriel was sent from God
to a town in Galilee called Nazareth,
with a message for a girl betrothed to a man named Joseph,
a descendant of David;
the girl's name was Mary.

From this part of the story we learn many things. The text is extremely careful to mention details, such as the particular town, Nazareth; the particular girl, Mary, betrothed to a particular man, Joseph. Their lineage is of David. All of this particularity is very important to establish Jesus' royal lineage. The name of the town, Nazareth, is important because of prophecies from the Hebrew Bible of this birth taking place there. Even the name of the angel is given, a particular herald of God, Gabriel.

With reference to our discernment themes, the particularity of the story offers a great message to us. As a person in discernment, your life with your particular circumstances, with your family history, your physical location, is all very important to God. Your particularity matters. Your individuality matters, as symbolized in your name. As we begin our prayerful discernment, I'll be asking you to listen again to your own particularity and your own name.

The angel went in and said to her,
"Greetings, most favored one! The Lord is with you."

Can you accept your own blessedness? Gabriel's first message to Mary is that she is favored. Our blessedness includes the potential of having our lives used in God's service.

But she was deeply troubled by what he said
and wondered what this greeting might mean.
Then the angel said to her,
"Do not be afraid, Mary, for God has been gracious to you;
you shall conceive and bear a son, and you shall give him the name Jesus.
He will be great; he will bear the title
'Son of the Most High';
the Lord God will give him the throne of his ancestor David,
and he will be king over Israel for ever;
his reign shall never end."

Mary is frightened. She offers us the very clear model of being honest with our emotions. Usually, there are aspects of fear associated with change. Mary's model encourages us to be very honest with our reactions.

The angel offers an explanation. Can we receive a similar message? That which is to be birthed through you will be for the health of the community? Perhaps, like Mary, you are receiving a summons from God that seems so great, that it's even more demanding than you had expected. If so, it's perfectly legitimate to ask questions, to seek clarity, and to listen for your fears and doubts.

"How can this be?" said Mary;
"[I am still a virgin]."

Here Mary shifts into a very practical consideration. How can this be? If you find yourself being asked to move into an area of inexperience, into a way of being for which you do not feel fully prepared, then state those doubts. Ask for clarification. Ask God to show the way.

The angel answered,
"The Holy Spirit will come upon you,
and the power of the Most High will overshadow you;
and for that reason the holy child to be born will be called,
'Son of God.'

This statement is perhaps the most significant of the story. If you are being asked by God for service, God will show a way. It may not come as quickly as you wish. It may not be given in the form you expected, but the way forward will be shown. And for this reason, you will be able to point to the leadership of the Holy Spirit in bringing about a resolution to your discernment.

> Moreover your kinswoman Elizabeth has herself
> conceived a son in her old age;
> and she who is reputed barren is now in her sixth month,
> for God's promises can never fail."

Finally, if your pathway is of God, you'll find others who are traveling the same road. The people equivalent to Elizabeth will begin to appear. You will have companions. Remember in our discussion of the hero/heroine's journey, helpers always appear in such stories. New helpers to assist this journey will come as well. It is very appropriate to ask God to show you who may be your helpers for this new task.

> "Here am I," said Mary;
> "I am the Lord's servant; as you have spoken, so be it."

Only after Mary has had her fears, her questions, and her doubts answered and only after she is given a companion in Elizabeth does she respond positively. Her story is a very helpful example of how to listen to our own hearts and how to listen to God. She does not immediately assent. She brings her unique humanness to the situation. She also has the strength of character to probe into the request with the angel. She inspires us to ask direct questions of God about the discernment issues before us.

> Then the angel left her.[7]

For the Discerner

I. Detail Your Progress

Perhaps you are beginning to come to clarity regarding the issue or issues you have posed for discernment. If you have not done so recently, now is a good time to review your responses to the exercises you've been doing until now in this discernment process. Perhaps in reading your previous responses you'll become clearer about the emerging discernment. Are there two or more options emerging for you? That would not be uncommon. Note these outcomes for discernment with as much attention to detail as possible.

2. Places and People to Visit

Are there particular places you need to visit in order to begin to be clearer about your decision? Do you need to schedule a trip to look into options? Are there particular individuals, particular helpers you need to engage in conversation about the emerging possibilities?

3. Schedule Retreat Time

If possible set aside a day for discernment or at least a half-day. If you are in a discerning process with your spouse, a business partner, or another person, try to schedule some retreat time together. Find a place that symbolizes a boundary place, in which you seem to listen well for God. Perhaps this is simply a favorite room in your home. Or perhaps you have a retreat place to which you go on occasion. Scheduling an overnight or day retreat at such a place can be very helpful for clarifying your direction.

4. Pray the Story of Mary

Enter into discernment through the story of Mary.

First of all spend time with the opening salutation. Hear God speaking your name, as spoken to Mary—hail most favored one (your name), the Lord is with you. Pray with this image until you sense your own blessedness. If you like, make a list of your blessings.

Then, begin to use the guidance of this chart to work through themes of the story. Receive your best guidance for outcomes as messages from God or from the angel calling you forth. If you have two options list them as outcome A and outcome B (or perhaps there are three options). For simplicity I'll use two in my guidance.

Name Outcome A Here	Name Outcome B Here
List pros and cons of this choice with as much detail as possible.	List pros and cons of this choice with as much detail as possible.
Review A and list your emotional responses to A.	Review B and list your emotional responses to B.

(continued on page 140)

(continued from page 139)

Review A and listen for your physiological responses. List those.	Review B and listen for your physiological responses. List those.
Review all of your responses in A and wait for an image or symbol capturing this outcome.	Review all of your responses in B and wait for an image or symbol capturing this outcome.

Center yourself in Christ or another Holy Guide.

Again receive the sense of your blessedness.

Offer each symbol or image to the Holy Guide one at a time.

Listen again for inner guidance and for your physical and emotional responses.

Note responses for outcome A. Note responses for outcome B.

Which answer makes your "heart sing for joy to the Lord?" Perhaps you've received a new answer as you've prayed over these possibilities.

Are there details you need to ask about? Remember Mary's astonishment that she was asked to be pregnant when she was a virgin. Here is a very good place to ask for specific help about how to accomplish what you believe you're being asked to do.

Who will be your helpers? From this place of prayer, you may receive very specific suggestions of people to contact to assist in your next steps of discernment.

---

5. Plans/Outcomes

Are there specific plans you can now create? Perhaps your outcome is that you have other information you need to gather. Perhaps there are other people you need to consult.

6. Resources

Refer to the information you have been gathering throughout your discernment process. Summarize these resources, compare these with what you've learned in the discernment of outcomes through the annunciation story. As you look over the things you have learned from this process, what areas of information gathering do you need to pursue now? Who are the people you need to consult?

7. Just for Fun

What is one thing you will do in the next week or two, just for fun? This can be very simple, such as going to lunch with a friend, taking a walk, going to a movie.

Name it _____ Schedule it _____

8. Practicalities

What information gathering, budget planning, conferring with others, etc., will you do now with reference to your discernment?

Refer to previous lists. What do you need to accomplish now?

Notes

1. Belden C. Lane, *The Solace of Fierce Landscapes: Exploring Desert and Mountain Spirituality* (New York and Oxford: Oxford University Press, 1998).

2. Ibid., 45, quoting from Robert L. Cohn, "Mountains in the Biblical Cosmos," *in The Shape of Sacred Space: Four Biblical Studies* (Chico, CA: Scholars Press, 1981), 26.

3. Lane, *Solace of Fierce landscapes*, 46.

4. David Abram, *The Spell of the Sensuous: Perception and Language in a More-Than-Human World* (New York: Pantheon Books, 1996).

5. Cf. Matt 1:20–21 and Luke 1:31–33 for these images.

6. For refreshing perspective on the gifts of aging, see William H. Thomas, *What Are Old People For? How Elders Will Save the World* (Acton, MA: VanderWyk & Burnham, 2004).

7. I am indebted to the work of Nicola Kester for these broad themes relating discernment to the story of the annunciation. See also Nicola Kester, "Meeting the Angel: The Annunciation as a Model of Personal Surrender" (PhD diss., Palo Alto, CA: Institute of Transpersonal Psychology, 1985).

11

Making a Plan:
Checking with Others

For everything there is a season,
and a time for every matter under heaven:
a time to be born, and a time to die;
a time to plant,
and a time to pluck up what is planted.
—Eccl: 3:1–2

Kaleidoscopic Views

The discernment journey has taken us into many domains of reflection. Each turn of the kaleidoscope has offered a different perspective on our current life transition. We've thought about life stages and how these may influence our decision process. We've explored the story-making patterns of the hero/heroine's journey and viewed our own life journey as a story. We've considered issues of location and embodiment. We've explored our relationship with God and our faith practices and how they are shifting in this time of transition. We've discussed how our own lives can play a part in God's work for shalom within the world. We may have worked deeply to find release from old patterns of hurt or pain that inhibit our being salt and light in the world. We've wondered about our geographical location for this next phase of life, as well as the balance of family considerations and personal calling. Perhaps clarity has begun to emerge.

Melissa had a successful career in curriculum development, then returned to graduate school for focusing in a new area. As she completed her master's degree the question of continuing studies with a doctoral program began to surface. On her discernment process, she commented: "It's always so fascinating to me how the whole discernment process works. I spent all summer thinking about it, writing, praying, journaling, etc., and then in the last month after leaving the question alone altogether—it just *settled* in my heart." Yes, that is what we are hoping to receive—the decision settling in our heart. As we think again on the kaleidoscopic perspective of our complex lives, perhaps our own discernment is beginning to settle. Here again is the dynamic pattern for our discernment issues:

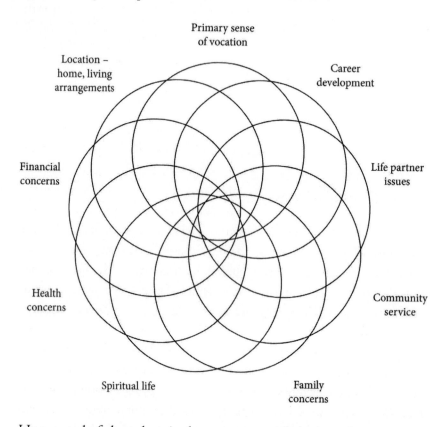

Have several of these domains become more settled in your heart?

Seasons of Life

As we continue to turn the kaleidoscope, various patterns emerge, all pro-foundly connected with one another. No matter which key area has been our place of beginning, each will be affected by our decisions. As we com-plete this journey of discernment, imagining our lives as seasons can be very helpful. Do our discernment decisions fit well with our season of life? We could think of our early childhood into late adolescence as winter, a time of rooting into life. During this period we are formed and nurtured by our families, schools, churches, and communities as well by as our rela-tionships with siblings and friends. We are unconsciously absorbing the great themes of our culture and of the particular times in which we have been born. Much growth takes place in our psychological and spiritual for-mation beneath the surface. Externally, we experience phenomenal growth physically, emotionally, and intellectually, while being formed in the soil of our culture. Internally much is occurring out of sight, our deep uncon-scious structures of personality are forming. In winter, the greatest growth is beneath the soil. Perhaps in our reflections we have discovered new insights into our roots, into this period of profound growth and personal-ity formation, or into wounds in need of healing.

Is it spring for you? Over the human life span we might well think of springtime as stretching from our late teens into our late thirties. It is the time of our first great movement into adulthood. Perhaps our springtime discernment issues are related to questions regarding life partner, marriage, or vocational choice. Perhaps the difficult balancing acts of vocation and parenthood have been the focus of our decision process. Perhaps the issue of whether or not to remain in a marriage relationship has been on our hearts. We may be struggling with a first career choice or may have hit the mid thirties question of whether we should shift vocational focus in a major way. It may be very difficult to begin to reflect seriously on a possibility of change-of-life focus when it has taken so very much energy to get to a state of stability. Even so, an underlying disquiet may have broken upon us. One partner in a relationship may have had a period of relative stability within vocation while the other is just completing a vocational preparation. Part-ners may need to renegotiate their present location, so that both can flourish in their next stage of career development. Spring is a time of rapid growth. It can feel like autumn is invading your season of growth when the summons of change comes upon you. This transition, however, can be in preparation for the coming summer in our forties, fifties, and sixties.

Summer is a critical time for making major contributions in our professional life. We may need to "catch up" with vocational aspirations in this season. We may have the opportunities to be stretched beyond our expectations in order to live into this great season of productivity. We may have suffered health or addiction problems that have interrupted this period of productivity. Summer may be a time marked by commitments to our families and careers that can be extremely demanding.

It is clear that I am beginning to look toward the autumn in my life. What would life mean if not so focused on responsibilities to career? In autumn there is much less to prove to others. There is more opportunity to allow our own personal interests to flourish again. Perhaps we can embrace our autumn as a season very similar to our springtime years. I've been getting a lot of positive energy thinking of my present interests much like undergraduate school again—a time to read widely, without the restraint of direct vocational interests; a time to renegotiate the meanings of being a global citizen; a time to explore interests widely. If we are entering autumn or if we are in autumn, do our aspirations and our energies match? Do we need to moderate our dreams based on a realistic assessment of physical stamina, health, or family concerns?

Finally, a second winter will arrive for us all. Perhaps part of our discernment process has been whether or not it is time to begin thinking about a retirement center for our latter years. Or perhaps we've been able to discern that we have too many more years of health and vigor to entertain such a change just yet. Perhaps we are thinking about moving to be nearer to adult children and grandchildren in preparation for the coming winter.

How marvelous it would be if we all were blessed with enough mental capacity to enter winter as a season of final blessing on our lives, offering amends as needed and blessing our children, grandchildren, and friends. Frequently, people in their autumn years begin writing personal memoires for their children and grandchildren, enlivened with photographs and stories of their life journeys. My wife's mother did this for her family. Then, when her memory diminished, she was the one comforted by the stories archived so lovingly in the scrapbooks she had prepared for others.

Leadership Diamond as Reference

The final model I would describe for our discernment is presented by philosopher Peter Koestenbaum in his book *Leadership: The Inner Side of Greatness, a Philosophy for Leaders.*[1] Koestenbaum offers a fourfold model for leadership. He names what he presents the Leadership Diamond.[2]

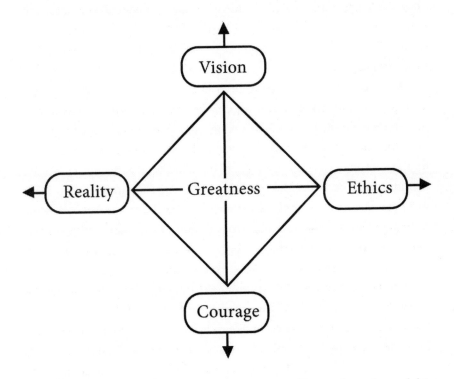

Written particularly for business executives, Koestenbaum's model is nonetheless very helpful to assist us in balancing our personality tendencies in any major decision process. Is our sense of Vision balanced by an appropriate sense of Reality? Or do we tend to be a bit too dreamy for our own good? Do we have grand ideas but difficulty translating them into effective action in the world? Do we have career aspirations but difficulty paying the bills? The Leadership Diamond helps us to see that Vision and

Reality must be kept in balance in order to fulfill our quest for meaning and service.

By Ethics, Koestenbaum means our sense of compassionate presence to others, our attention to human concerns. For many of us our sense of care for family members (Ethics) is very likely to come into conflict at some point with our career Vision. Our decisions to assist aging parents may be in direct conflict with vocational choices. We may see little way beyond such an impasse. The Leadership Diamond encourages us not to collapse such difficult tensions too easily. Instead, we are encouraged to live into these deep dilemmas until resolution emerges. Finally, Koestenbaum speaks of Courage. We may have wonderful Vision for our discernment and still stumble on necessary acts of Courage to venture forth into the new adventure calling to us.

Throughout my career, I've been extraordinarily privileged to walk alongside people making major life changes. I've observed courageous acts in seemingly simple gestures, like taking a graduate course after a hiatus of twenty or more years since academic study. I've seen people move from place to place, inspired by divine calling. I've observed people staying in place for considerations of family. Joseph Campbell's hero/heroine's journey helps us in our quest for appropriate Courage. If you think you truly are being summoned into a new life quest that requires new sources of Courage, remember to reach out to the new helpers for this life journey who may be presenting themselves. Perhaps we end this time of discernment with the need for some Courage partners to assist us. Perhaps we end this time of discernment with clarity that we need some Reality partners. We may see that our skills are not in marketing ourselves or in financial administration, for example, and we determine to seek some people to be team members with us in a new venture. It can be a great relief for us to pay attention to that which is truly our giftedness and to seek helpers to strengthen us.

Koestenbaum's model is very helpful in showing us our tendencies. We all have what Koestenbaum describes as a collapsed Leadership Diamond. Our basic personality may look like any of these collapsed diamonds.[3]

In Person a, Vision, Reality, and Courage are strong, but Ethics is very weak. This would be a person who does not consider the effects of deci-

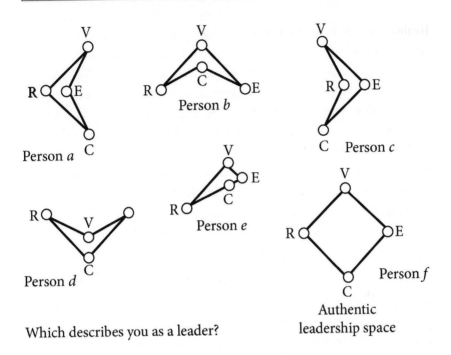

Person a

Person b

Person c

Person d

Person e

Person f

Authentic
leadership space

Which describes you as a leader?

sions on others. What does your collapsed Leadership Diamond usually look like? As you face this time of discernment, look for the traps that are unique to your strengths and weaknesses in the areas of: Vision, Reality, Ethics, and Courage. What kinds of help do you need to balance your natural tendencies? Does your discernment stretch you in all of these dimensions or assist you to become more balanced?

Koestenbaum writes of the "inner side of greatness," illustrating the difficulty of seeking to keep our Leadership Diamond stretching in each of the domains. Craig Emerick, a discernment colleague of mine for many years, introduced me to Koestenbaum's work. Craig speaks of the interior of the Leadership Diamond as the domain of "soulfulness" rather than "mindfulness," the term used by Koestenbaum.[4] Craig is pointing to the need for creating the inner spaciousness and mystery of life along with the skills of Vision, Ethics, Reality, and Courage. Soulfulness points us toward the need to continue to increase in wisdom throughout our lives. Are we able over our life spans and in this particular season of discernment to pray

through our areas of needed personal growth? Can we seek our answers
with the trust that "all things work together for good for those who love
God, who are called according to [God's] purpose" (Rom 8:28)?

Perhaps this season of discernment is one in which God's purposes are
pressing upon you with new urgency and you are being pushed to increase
your capacities in one or more areas described by the Leadership Diamond.
Perhaps you need a season of prayer to increase your capacities for service
and leadership before you are clear about new directions. Perhaps God is
summoning you to respond as did Mary, "Here am I; . . . I am the Lord's
servant; as you have spoken, so be it"(Luke 1:38).

For the Discerner—Reviewing Your Decisions

By now I hope some decisions have been clarified. Perhaps you've gotten a very
clear idea of a plan for action. Or you've learned that it is not yet time to
complete this decision process. Either outcome is good. In our decision
processes, there is a time for action and a time for further reflection. The wisdom of Ecclesiastes helps us. In the midst of major decisions, there is often
a conviction of absolute clarity for me on one issue, but a month or two later
other realities have resurfaced regarding the decision and it must be reconsid-
ered. It's messy sometimes, but giving our major decisions time to evolve is
vital. Perhaps your best use of this book is to set aside your reflections for
another season and then pick them up again for further consideration. Or
perhaps the time is at hand to move on with the insights you've gained.

Perhaps you've been visited by dreams during this discernment time. Or
you've had particularly clear nudges in your prayer time. Now is a good time
to review all of these promptings and seek to discern which ones are truly
of the Holy Spirit. For example, profound fear can sometimes surface in
the midst of a decision process. Is this fear a result of a way of being that
you are called to leave behind or is it a result of caution? You may need to
pray further over such major themes that have emerged.

I. Review Your Work
   Review your journal notes, dreams, and prayer experiences over the
   period of your discernment. Review your notes, in particular, from the

discernment process with Mary's story in chapter 10, and issues that emerged for further review.

2. Live with Your Outcomes

If you still have more than one outcome emerging within your discernment, "live" with each of these outcomes for a week at a time. Extend your discernment time over the next month. During the week that you "live" with each outcome, pay special attention to your emotional responses, to your sense of creativity, and to your concerns over particular details. That week should be as focused as possible on taking on that particular outcome. Then, shift your focus to the other outcome the next week. Notice which outcome seems to "settle in your heart."

3. Make an Action Plan

Be as clear as you can. Utilize the broad themes of life's seasons to help you understand the appropriateness of your plans. Utilize the Leadership Diamond as a sounding board for your decision process. Are you paying proper attention to each of the four domains, Vision, Reality, Ethics, and Courage? What practical steps evolve as you work with each domain? As you live into realities of your decision process, you'll often discover that the greater realities of the world help shift your expectations. Can you undertake this engagement with the world's realities as an adventure? Are you ready to have your own sense of life calling adjusted by what you encounter? Are you ready to allow the Holy Spirit to guide in the realities you encounter in your attempt to live into this decision?

4. Check with Others

It's critical to confer with people affected by your decision process. They now become part of your Reality dimension of your Diamond. Do they also sense with you that this is the right decision? What questions do they raise?

5. Check with Christ

Read the Beatitudes (Matt 5:1–14). In what ways is your decision consistent with Christ's hopes for a world of peace and justice?

Notes

1. Peter Koestenbaum, *Leadership, the Inner Side of Greatness: A Philosophy for Leaders* (San Francisco: Jossey-Bass, 2002).

2. Ibid., 18. Used with permission of the publisher.

3. Ibid., 188. Used with permission of the publisher.

4. Personal communication with Rev. Craig L. Emerick, DMin, Emerick and Associates, Dallas, TX, 2000.

Afterword

This time of discernment has been a time of prayerfulness, a time for listening to longings, aspirations, hopes, and realities. It has been a time for listening for your *vocatio*, your inner voice prompting you to endings and new beginnings. Transitions are filled with hope and fear, with joy and difficulties. Through this time of prayerful reflection, I hope you have found new listening partners who inspire you. I hope you have found a new depth of affirmation of your inner strength for significant decisions, as well as strategies to deal with the inevitable problems that emerge. I hope you end this time of reflection with a deepened conviction that God is with you, whatever the particular outcome of your discernment. I pray that you have discovered something deep at work within your present life transition— God's own work within you expanding your heart in compassion and in joy. For this continuing work, I leave you with this blessing:

> I pray that your inward eyes may be illumined,
> so that you may know what is the hope to which [God] calls you . . .
> and how vast the resources of [God's] power open to us who trust in him.

—EPHESIANS I:18–19 (NEB)

May it be so for you now and in future seasons of discernment.

Bibliography

Abram, David. *The Spell of the Sensuous: Perception and Language in a More-Than-Human World.* New York: Pantheon Books, 1996.

Achterberg, Jeanne. *Lightning at the Gate: A Visionary Journey of Healing.* Boston: Shambhala, 2002.

Andras, Joan. "A Phenomenological Investigation of The Decision-process of a Woman Trusting Herself in Making a Spiritual Commitment That is Contrary to the Wishes of a Significant Person or Persons." PhD diss., Palo Alto, CA: Institute of Transpersonal Psychology, 1993.

Beckman, Betsey, and Christine Valter Painters. *Awakening the Creative Spirit: Bringing the Arts to Spiritual Direction.* New York: Church Publishing, Morehouse, 2010.

Blum, Deborah. *Sex on the Brain: The Biological Differences between Men and Women.* New York: Penguin Putnam, 1997.

Bly, Robert. *Iron John: A Book about Men.* Reading, MA: Addison-Wesley, 1990.

Bohler, Carolyn Stahl. *Opening to God: Guided Imagery Meditation on Scripture.* Nashville: Upper Room Books, 1996.

Boyer, Jr., Ernest. *A Way in the World: Family Life as Spiritual Discipline.* San Francisco: Harper & Row, 1984; paperback edition, *Finding God at Home: Family Life as Spiritual Discipline.* New York: HarperCollins, 1988.

Bridges, William. *Transition: Making Sense of Life's Changes.* 2nd ed. Cambridge, MA: DaCapo Press, Perseus Books, 2004.

Campbell, Joseph. *The Hero with a Thousand Faces.* 2nd ed. Princeton, NJ: Princeton University Press, Bollingen Foundation, Inc., 1968.

———. *The Masks of God,* Vol iv: *Creative Mythology.* New York, Viking, 1968.

Cohen, Gene D. *The Mature Mind: The Positive Power of the Aging Brain.* New York: Basic Books, 2006.

Cohn, Robert L. "Mountains in the Biblical Cosmos," *The Shape of Sacred Space: Four Biblical Studies*. Chico, CA: Scholars Press, 1981.

Dossey, Larry. *Healing Words: The Power of Prayer and the Practice of Medicine*. San Francisco: HarperSanFrancisco, 1993.

Erikson, Erik H. *Identity and the Life Cycle*. New York: Norton, 1980

———. *Life Cycle Completed, Extended Version with New Chapters on the Ninth Stage of Development by Joan M. Erikson*. New York: Norton, 1997.

Fox, Matthew. *Breakthrough: Meister Eckhart's Creation Spirituality in New Translation*. Garden City, NY: Doubleday, Image Books, 1980.

———. *Original Blessing: A Primer in Creation Spirituality Presented in Four Paths, Twenty-Six Themes, and Two Questions*. New York: Tarcher/Putnam, 2000.

Gilligan, Carol. *In a Different Voice: Psychological Theory and Women's Development*. Cambridge, MA: Harvard University Press, 1982, 1993.

Haid, Richard, and Caitlin Williams, eds. "Counseling for the Third Quarter of Life." Special issue, *Career Planning and Adult Development Journal* (San Jose, CA: Career Planning and Adult Development Network) 15, no.3, fall 1999).

"Healing Services and Prayers, Introduction," *The United Methodist Book of Worship*. Nashville: The United Methodist Publishing House, 1992.

Hillman, James. *The Soul's Code: In Search of Character and Calling*. New York: Random House, 1996.

Holmes, Barbara. *Joy Unspeakable: Contemplative Practices of the Black Church*. Minneapolis: Fortress Press, 2004.

Holy Bible: King James Version. Nashville: Thomas Nelson, 2004.

Holy Bible: New Revised Standard Version. Grand Rapids, MI: Zondervan, 1993.

Kester, Nicola. "Meeting the Angel: The Annunciation as a Model of Personal Surrender." PhD diss. Palo Alto, CA: Institute of Transpersonal Psychology, 1985.

Koestenbaum, Peter. *Leadership, the Inner Side of Greatness: A Philosophy for Leaders*. San Francisco: Jossey-Bass, 2002.

Lane, Belden C. *The Solace of Fierce Landscapes: Exploring Desert and Mountain Spirituality*. New York and Oxford: Oxford University Press, 1998.

Levinson, Daniel J., with Charlotte N. Darrow, Edward B. Klein, Maria H.Levinson, Braxton McKee. *The Seasons of a Man's Life*. New York: Ballantine Books, 1978.

Mellick, Jill. *The Art of Dreaming: Tools for Creative Dream Work*. Berkeley: Conari, 1996.

New English Bible. New York, Cambridge University Press, 1971.

Palmer, Parker J. *Let Your Life Speak: Listening for the Voice of Vocation*. San Francisco: Jossey-Bass, 2000.

Peck, M.D., M. Scott. *The Road Less Traveled, 25th Anniversary Edition: A New Psychology of Love, Traditional Values and Spiritual Growth*. New York, Touchstone, 2003.

Potter, Beverly A. *The Way of the Ronin: Riding the Waves of Change*. Berkeley, CA: Ronin Publishing, 1984, 2001.

Ruffing, Janet K. *Spiritual Direction: Beyond the Beginnings*. New York: Paulist Press, 2000.

Schachter-Shalomi, Zalman, and Ronald S. Miller. *From Age-ing to Sage-ing: A Profound New Vision of Growing Older*. New York: Warner Books, 1995.

Sheehy, Gail. *Passages: Predictable Crises of Adult Life*. New York: Dutton, 1974, 1976.

————. *New Passages: Mapping Your Life across Time*. New York: Ballantine, 1995.

Smith, Huston. *The World's Religions*. San Francisco: HarperSanFrancisco, 1991.

Snyder, Chase. "Changing Direction: Mike Miller, 30, is one of many in this area who is using the economic downturn as an opportunity to better themselves," *Goshen (IN) News*, Working Together section, February 17, 2009.

Taylor, Jeremy. *Where People Fly and Water Runs Uphill: Using Dreams to Tap the Wisdom of the Unconscious*. New York: Warner Books, 1992.

Teilhard de Chardin, Pierre. *The Making of a Mind: Letters from a Soldier-Priest, 1914–1919*, trans. R. Hague. London: Collins, 1965.

Thomas, William H. *What Are Old People For? How Elders Will Save the World*. Acton, MA: VanderWyk & Burnham, 2004.

Thompson, Marjorie. *Soul Feast: An Invitation to the Christian Spiritual Life*. Louisville, KY: Westminster John Knox Press, 1995.

The United Methodist Hymnal, Book of United Methodist Worship. Nashville: The United Methodist Publishing House, 1989.

Viorst, Judith. *Necessary Losses: The Loves, Illusions, Dependencies, and Impossible Expectations That All of Us Have to Give Up in Order to Grow*. New York: Fireside, 1986, 1998.

von Franz, M.-L. "The Process of Individuation," *Man and His Symbols*. Edited by Carl G. Jung. New York: Dell, 1968.

Wade, Jenny. *Changes of Mind: A Holonomic Theory of the Evolution of Consciousness*. Albany, NY: State University of New York Press, 1996.